RUFFLED BUTTERFLIES

RUFFLED
BUTTERFLIES

AYOTUNDE MAMUDU

origami

Parrésia Publishers Ltd.
82, Allen Avenue, Ikeja, Lagos, Nigeria.
+2348154582178, +2348062392145
origami@parresia.com.ng
www.parresia.com.ng

ISBN: 978-978-55874-7-0

Printed in Nigeria by Parrésia Press

FOR

The memory of my father, Professor Ayo Mamudu and my mother Mrs Julie Mamudu, the strongest woman on earth. God bless you, Mummy. This is also for Jesse, Ifeoluwa and Rinret.

DISCLAIMER

This work is fictional, any resemblance of names, characters, businesses, events, locales, and incidents are either the products of the author's imagination or used in a fictitious manner. Any resemblance to actual persons, living or dead, or actual events is purely coincidental.

CONTENTS

TOOTHPASTE

How can where I squeeze the toothpaste tube summarise who I am, and form an opinion to the entire clan from which I wrestled their son? The thought bugs me as I drive back from the corner shop near the junction. Is this idea of defining someone by a single action, or even of toothpaste, African? Kai! I wonder what books or websites my husband gets his ideas from. As if it is not my husband, the same one I visited when he stayed with his mother in that house behind Mechanic Village.

'Babe, you really shouldn't strangle the toothpaste tube,' he would say in a high-nosed I-lived-in-Buckingham palace, trained-by-three-special-butlers-on-squishing-toothpaste way. This toothpaste affair started like a joke after we got married and we had both laughed about it. But it soon took on an attitude of disgruntlement: my husband felt I did not appreciate his efforts at brushing me up.

This morning, I had looked forward to dinner: my husband and I planned to host a little affair. It was a get-together to celebrate life with loved ones; so, the guest list was carefully drawn to include a few family members and some of our very good friends. I started cooking early in the morning, so that I would have ample time to rest and soak in the tub before guests arrive. But I didn't find the time to soak in the tub. We ran out of cooking gas and I had to run for a refill. I don't like carrying the cylinder because, well, it is a man's job. But the idea of scrubbing pots after cooking on a kerosene stove did not appeal to me. So, I quickly hauled the gas cylinder to the station. I have always wondered why no one has invented a gas app that could be downloaded from Google Play Store because, you see, gas has a mind of its own. It runs out intentionally on Saturday evenings or Sunday mornings when it's almost impossible to get a refill. On my way back from the gas station, Folake, my dear friend – I always call her Flakey – called to say she was coming over to help with the cooking; I was pleased. Flakey is a complete package – help and company.

Earlier this week, my husband told me that he would not be home to help because his business associates were in town. He had to show them around to see the state of things and tour the farm where he worked, carrying out cutting edge research in plant genetics. Research which his associates sponsored. I told him not to worry, all he had to do was arrive on time.

Flakey and I fried, grilled, boiled, stewed, roasted, baked, pureed, grated and sweated all day. Towards evening, about an hour before our guests were due to arrive, everything finally looked perfect. The salad looked like we had played with colours, the prawns and roast chicken looked like they were having a fellowship and the pepper-soup announced itself by silently assaulting the nose. And of course, fish and chips; I couldn't do a get-together without fish and chips. The house was spotlessly clean; Flakey and I just needed to shower. I only started to shower when I suddenly remembered that we did not have enough fuel in our generator – a power cut would ruin the evening – so I dashed out, again.

It seemed our guests timed themselves because they all arrived around 7:30 pm. My husband hadn't come. I called his cell phone twice and got a text message from him: *around the koner, can smell your fish n chips.* The noise from our generator was loud, and our TV was doing a valiant job outdoing it. Our guests spoke in a louder voice. On the TV, the news feature was about Nigerians returning from Libya. Most of them concealed their faces from the flash photographs and inquisitive journalists: 'Were you into prostitution in Libya? How were you ferried off into the trade, is there a ringleader?' No one paid any attention to the TV – we were busy greeting one another.

It was good to see everyone, especially those who lived within the neighbourhood and who we never saw except when they drove by. It seemed like the past few months had passed, and we were yet to live the time. 'Are we now so busy?' Charlotte asked Temi, who she had just hugged. 'We barely see each other these days.' Temi smiled.

Since no one minded the TV, I decided to turn it down and put on some music. I was about to touch the TV when a voice boomed: 'Can you please tune the TV to SuperSport 5? There is a championship match today.' It was Johnson, Temi's husband; he spoke from the other end of the room where he was with the boys – Okhues, Meata and Ochai. The others had yet to come. 'You have SuperSport 5, right?' I replied that we did. All the men in the room suddenly spoke up. 'Yeah, yeah, let's watch the match.' It seemed like they had all been waiting for someone to speak up.

My husband was yet to arrive and '*around the koner, can smell your fish n chips*' kept ringing in my head. I knew that a toddler pushing a tricycle would not spend an hour – it had been an hour since his text came in – coming home from around the corner. I had just glanced at the wall clock for the umpteenth time when he came in still wearing his jacket and tightly knotted polka dot tie, like he wanted me to believe he had been working till he stepped into the house. Once he stepped in, a cheer went up. The cheer that greeted his arrival felt strange: it sounded like everyone was praising him for setting up such a wonderful evening. What did he do? I fumed inwardly. I managed to corner him in the hallway just before our bedroom and asked in a suppressed angry voice: 'Where have you been?' He stepped back, took in my light blue gown and a soft boyfriend jacket and said, 'I am here now, Babe.' He smiled and stepped into the bedroom. I thought I smelled cigarette smoke on him, but I also knew he didn't smoke. The way he said *I am here now, Babe* took me back across space and time, to a not-so distant memory.

I met Kayode Thomas in Kano during my NYSC year. I grew up in Lagos and schooled there all my life. So, while waiting to be called up, I already knew I would be sent far from home. When I got posted to Kano State, I was not surprised or sad; only scared. I had never been to the North; in fact, I had never travelled so far away from home. But I had heard all the news of violence happening in the North. I chose to go because I knew I would not be alone. So, I travelled to Kano by air and took a cab to the orientation camp. We must have been the highest number of corps members a batch had ever seen, because it took forever to get our paperwork done. When the paperwork was done, we settled for life on camp which began immediately.

On the first full day of camp, I was really tired after a day of marching in the sun and just wanted to get back to the hostel room I shared with nineteen other girls. Once I entered the room, I noticed that my bag was smaller. It was exactly in the same place and position I had left it, but it was smaller. The lock was still in place and had not been touched. When I turned the bag, I saw a neat long incision on its side. Someone had cut my bag with a razor and stolen what he wanted. What remained were photocopies of my school credentials. My name, Olabisi Akinbolu, boldly typed and, in another paper, beautifully calligraphed, was visible in the darkening twilight. Whoever stole my things had taken his or her time to prop the four corners inside the bag with sticks. Four of us in the room discovered this almost at the same time. Everything, even my underwear, was gone. Who did this? What kind of mischief went on in the fellow's head? Thankfully, I had my money in my black waist pouch, or I would have been stranded.

That night, the girls in my dorm came up with a thousand ways to recover our stolen items. One girl said if we all stood naked outside the dorm at 1 am and cursed the thief, he would bring our things back within the week. I thought that was funny. Anger and grief could do funny things to the mind and make one do desperate, if not foolish, things. One girl beside me muttered that she had never heard such BS in her life. I don't think the others heard her. I simply thought that our things had been stolen, and there really was nothing we could do about it, except make a report. But who made a report about stolen panties?

The next morning, I went to the mammy-market to buy some underwear. I did not bother with clothes since I could make do with the uniforms provided by the scheme. I looked at some flimsy pieces the shop owner showed me, swearing they were all original from America. 'My brother just travel come back. Direct America. Follow come,' he bragged. But I could see the labels: 'Guccee,' 'LF,' 'Tonni Hilfinger'. They were underwear in any case, so I bought a few. When I stepped out of the shop, I saw a young man strangely wearing panties on his head and hanging a huge leaf green brassiere around his neck. He called himself 'Pant and Bra Thief.' He sat close to some other corps members who were eating breakfast at a nearby *mai shayi*.

Pant and Bra Thief had an audience that laughed really hard. He teased some girls in the group for not having dignified underwear. If they did, it should have had the honour of being stolen. He said they wore boxers instead. I laughed. I remembered my turquoise lace trimmed Victoria Secrets which were gone; they still had the tags on them. I also remembered some girls back in my school who wore Jeans trousers and pulled them down to expose their G-strings. 'If you bought them for that price, you have to flaunt them,' they'd said often.

Later that evening, when I did not feel like eating the NYSC mass-produced yam porridge, I went down to the mammy-market for some bread, eggs and suya. Getting to the mai shayi, I saw Pant and Bra Thief serving out tea in plastic cups. He had, in just two days, built a rapport with the owners of the shop and helped them out. I still wonder why. There was this way the mai shayi cooled the tea. He would pour out tea from one cup into another, while increasing the distance between both cups. It looked like pouring glue because the tea never spilled. Pant and Bra Thief had also perfected this art to the amazement of his friends who all watched in awe as I waited for someone to take my order. I must have zoned out, because when Pant and Bra Thief touched me, I startled; he was calm: 'I am here now, Babe,' he said and took my order.

When I returned to the living room, the men had formed an arch in front of the TV; the football game had started. All the guys had their coaching ideas and were very quick to shout at the TV or groan when a player had not done what they 'asked' him to do. I marvelled at the energy these men put into the game. I had seen it many times; my Kayode wasn't any different. He was never to be disturbed during a football game. My warnings that our baby would wake up were not always enough to keep him from shouting coaching advice at the screen or, sometimes, cursing the referee for what he felt was an unfair decision. And when his team scored, his voice joined the echo on the street shouting 'gooooooal'.

Our party did not need formal introductions or speeches, so food was served right away. At a corner, I noticed two very beautiful young women who didn't mix either because they were not familiar or they really loved checking all the pictures on their phones for the umpteenth time. I wasn't sure if they came with Daniel, my brother in-law; or Oyi, our neighbour. Both men were married the last time I checked. Instead of just wondering, I walked up to the girls to find out, suspecting they were my husband's guests. As I stretched my hand to introduce myself to them, Kayode, my husband, asked me for the cork screw. I left for the kitchen smiling and looking at both girls. 'I'll be right back,' I mouthed. The presence of both girls felt sour, like the aftertaste of bad wine.

'Goooooooooooooal! I said it, I said it.' The tension that accompanied the football game had burst into excitement. Some of the guys were running around the living room. We women mostly looked amused but did not join in the mayhem. Of course, a few of us were interested. Helen, who Kayode and I had not seen for about five months, actually hi-fived her husband. From the corner of my eye, I caught one of the young girls tapping my husband's left shoulder, as if she was congratulating him and his team for the goal. His team wasn't even playing that night. I looked at the corkscrew in my hand and smiled. I love it when a piano or an elephant would fall on a character in a cartoon. I imagined the corkscrew evolving into one of the Transformers or Voltron, brandishing his blazing sword to ward off the girls from my husband. The corkscrew actually looked like one of the Transformers when the handle was twisted and the wings lifted.

I had not eaten; I had only had a few drinks. I wasn't hungry, perhaps because I tasted too much of the food when Flakey and I were cooking. Our guests seemed to enjoy the food. Why wouldn't they? I thought. It was free. Suddenly, I began to wonder why everyone had accepted our invitation. But I knew that our friends were not really my problem, Kayode was. He was the one making my thoughts run in circles.

I went into the room to make sure my baby, Oreoluwa, was sleeping. Oreoluwa was with Grandma and Grandpa in their room. My parents-in-law had lived with us for some time.

'Well done, our daughter,' Grandpa said when I came in. He sat in a chair just by the door, while Grandma was settled on the bed opposite where I was. Satisfied that my baby had not been disturbed by all the excitement, I made to return to the living room.

'Bisi,' Grandma called.

'Ma,' I answered.

'Sit,' she said.

It suddenly occurred to me that I was standing between my parents-in-law, and that the arrangement was perfect for a confrontation. I sat.

'Bisi,' Grandma called, 'what is happening between you and Kayode?'

I was shocked by this question. My husband and I had mostly been at peace. We did not have any more issues than any normal couple. A complaint here, a grumble there, nothing serious; we never even got to the point of yelling at each other. I replied that we did not have any issues.

'Are you sure?'

'Yes Mama, nothing.'

I sat, head bowed and was thinking what this was about when Grandma started talking. She talked about how peace in any home was the function of the woman, and how she was to be held responsible if the ambience of the house had gone sour. I simply answered, 'Yes ma,' or 'No ma' as was needed, but my heart was not there. I was wondering which one of the phone-pressing, long-stretched-extension-wearing girls was responsible for this talk. Grandma was saying that her son was not happy, and she hoped I would find a solution soon. My thoughts ran in a widening gyre. Why should I be responsible for the happiness of a grown man? I was responsible for his feeding, his clothes, and now his happiness? But I kept my thoughts to myself and listened. Grandpa was silent; he mostly was. But I somehow felt he was in on whatever the issue was. I was getting ready to thank Grandma and plead with her to simply tell me what I needed to do when Kayode bustled in.

'Babe, could you please help me…'

He didn't finish the sentence, a part of me thought he wanted to ask me to line the toilet seat with tissue paper, so his girlfriend could gingerly perch and take a dunk. He paused as he entered the room. I looked at him, a question in my eyes – what was going on? Did he set his parents up to this?

Kayode was silent for a while, then he blurted, 'Mama she also squeezes the toothpaste from the neck.'

Something happened to the air in the room; it suddenly felt like I was breathing in ground peppers. But I neither choked nor said a thing. I never ever blew up in front of family or friends whenever

Kayode and I rowed. It was Kayode I had a problem with, and it was with him I would trash it. He stood there by the door while his mother started all over again on all the things I should do. Did I not know that the way I squeezed toothpaste said a lot about who I was? I sat, head bowed, trying to recall what Kayode had said about 'What your toothpaste says about you.' First, there was the category of people who squeezed the tube from the middle. Those who rolled up the bottom of the tube, making sure every bit was used up and the tube did not take up space in the cabinet. And then, there was the category of people who squeezed the toothpaste from the neck. Under the barrage from Grandma, I couldn't figure out where I belonged and how it mattered. I just thought that if my husband had a problem with something I did or didn't do, he should have told me about it. If he couldn't tell me about it, then it wasn't worth it.

I tried to figure out what the real problem was because I was sure it wasn't about how I squeezed the toothpaste tube. The other day, when we went to the zoo, I saw two baboons kiss. A girl asked her mother, 'Mummy, do baboons brush their teeth?' It was a hilarious question, but the recollection made me think. Was my husband interested in my dentition and hoped my teeth would not fall out before I got to thirty-five and embarrass him in public? I could always get artificial teeth. Some very fancy white and nicely trimmed teeth. And then I would talk with my teeth clenched like one of those models with plastic smiles. Or did I have bad breath? I blew hard on the back of my hand and sniffed my breath just to confirm. I had recently started brushing my teeth twice a day – when I did not forget or sleep off in front of the TV.

Kayode and I went back to the living room to join our guests. There was an electric boogaloo train going around the living room. Someone had put on some old soul train break dance music and waists were held forming a train of dancers. We loved to dance, Kayode and me. We quickly joined the dance and rocked. Stopped. Popped. Broke down. Came alive. In no time we were sweaty all over.

Kayode and I really rocked the clubs in our NYSC days. I remember this party we had once where we danced to the amazement of the entire crowd. They formed a ring around us and watched us do our thing. We discovered a lot of things in common back in Kano and consolidated on them in Lagos. We were inseparable and decided to get married.

The party began to break up as people started leaving. Everyone thanked us for the food and wonderful evening; they hoped we would do this again sometime soon. We replied that we hoped to always have a reason to celebrate life. As we chatted a bit outside, saying goodbye to the last of our friends, I saw Richard in a tight embrace with one of the young girls behind my car. Richard was my cousin who lived in our boy's quarters. The second pair of tightly hugged bodies was Doyin and the second smallie – Doyin was Richards' course-mate at the University.

When our guests had all gone, I drove out to the single shop 'supermarket' near our estate gate. My head was filled with thoughts of me and my siblings helping our father prepare his special chewing stick. I bought a six-in-one pack of toothpaste – with one free, and headed back home. The photo-shopped couple with their artificial smile on the pack annoyed me a little. But I was really thinking, 'How can where I squeeze the toothpaste tube summarise who I am, and form an opinion to the entire clan from which I wrestled their son?'

Home now. I park the car and walk past the front door into the store, a separate building outside the house. I pick a cutlass and walk into my small garden where I grow vegetables and most of my pepper soup ingredients. I start digging up the roots of one of the bitter leaf trees. I know my husband is peeping through the curtains, but I don't mind. After getting a few long tender roots, I set up a small fire using paper and kerosene to keep the fire going. I gradually roast the roots, scraping off the black burnt bark with a small knife. I can feel Kayode's piercing gaze, but I really don't care. Done, I walk into the house, straight to the bathroom where Kayode is brushing his teeth before going to bed. I stack the six-in-one toothpaste pack in the small cabinet and put my freshly roasted bitter leaf roots in a small cup just beside the toothpaste. I will not say a word to Kayode. I'm going to bed.

END

PUT THE TOILET SEAT DOWN

Amaka stood looking down the toilet bowl. Her cheeks were puffed, and her breathing was laboured. Tears gradually welled up in her eyes and slid down her cheeks and she made no move to wipe them. She was alone. She stood in the bathroom in her fluffy, sparkling white towel which covered her breasts and fell to her thighs. From the bathroom, she could see Ehigie's blue C320 Mercedes as he reversed from the car port. The front gate slid open, and he was off.

The cause of Amaka's worry was going away without acknowledging that he had caused a problem. She had told him many times to make sure that what he flushed was completely gone before he left the bathroom. Her blurred gaze was now directed at the floating brown clumps bobbing up and down like a lifebuoy at sea. Sometime in the previous week, Amaka had dragged Ehigie into the bathroom and showed him his lunch in the toilet bowl: un-chewed corn and bits of vegetable.

'Honey, when you use the toilet and flush, please wait for the cistern to refill and flush again before you leave or fill a bucket with water from the bathtub and pour directly into the toilet bowl to flush everything.' Amaka had demonstrated while she said this. She flushed, fetched water from the sink into a bucket and flushed again. Ehigie had said 'sorry' and 'okay' and returned to what he was doing.

Amaka did not like her husband's bathroom habits. She knew that if she was going to live with him for the rest of her life, she had to let him know. They had been living together for six months, after a very showy wedding. The wedding could not have been different because Ehigie rolled with the political elite. He called himself 'The Hill in Ikpoba,' and all his friends simply called him 'The Hill'.

Two weeks after their wedding, Amaka and Ehigie moved into their three-bedroom apartment. The place, situated in a highbrow area of their city, was beautiful. Amaka supervised the painting and interior decoration herself; so, the colours, curtains and tiles were all done to a perfect finish. A week after they moved in, Ehigie went for a political meeting and returned late at night. His movements woke Amaka from sleep, but she laid with her eyes closed, willing herself back to sleep. She could hear him urinating in the bathroom for a long while. He must have had a lot to drink, she thought. The next morning when she got up to use the bathroom; she was appalled to see yellow stains on the floor tiles and toilet seat. It was as if he had just stood by the door and aimed his pee at the toilet bowl. She cleaned the place and blamed the urine on the alcohol.

Amaka did not like to see Ehigie's hair in the washbasin. She loved his Afro which he trimmed every weekend and occasionally combed throughout the day. She liked that he used some of her hair treatment lotion which gave his hair sheen under the sun. She liked that her friends admired her husband's hair, especially her friends who had a hard time maintaining their natural hair. Their hair was not just right despite all the expensive stuff they bought and applied.

Amaka had a friend, Chibututu, who was totally in awe of Ehigie's hair; she always talked of burying her fingers in his Afro. Amaka often laughed and said she hoped her friend was not after the man under the hair. She once threatened to cut off the hair while Ehigie was asleep if Chibututu did not restrain herself. Both friends had laughed at this.

Ehigie always looked like a revolutionary black movement activist because of his hair, especially when he wore his black rimmed glasses and trench coat. Amaka loved the look, but she also knew that hair like that came with responsibilities. She decided to get a standing mirror in the bedroom since Ehigie combed his hair in front of the small mirror just over the wash hand basin leaving strands of hair in the toothbrush cup and basin, enough to clog the drain. The standing mirror came bordered with thick dark brown oak and could reveal her entire body. Ehigie could comb and pat his hair all he wanted without leaving hair in the wash hand basin for her to clean up afterwards. Amaka didn't mind sweeping the room, so far as she didn't have to get a plumber to harvest hairlocks and grime from the drain.

As Amaka watched Ehigie's blue C320 Mercedes drive out of the compound, she pulled herself together and had her bath; she resolved to talk to Ehigie in the evening. That evening, she served him dinner and watched him eat. As he ate, he asked about her day and told her about his; he told her of his progress on a business pitch he had made. It was huge, he said, and things could only get better. He also swore that she was the charm that brought him all the good luck. He left her a piece of meat on his plate, saying she was the baby of the house. Amaka laughed and cleared the dishes; she washed them and joined him in the living room. Ehigie was watching a basketball game and Amaka thought to leave him alone.

But she knew he would not see the end of the game because he would start dozing in about twenty minutes. It was best she spoke with him immediately.

'Darling, what do I have to do to make you flush the toilet properly,' she asked while caressing his ear lobe.

Ehigie fixed his wife a blank stare. 'You know, if you could just take down your panties from the handlebar of my treadmill, then maybe we could start talking about toilet ethics.'

His reply was sharp, delivered in a voice of steel. Amaka was not just startled; she was pierced. Where had all that venom come from?

Ehigie loved to workout: he did not want to have a beer pregnancy. So, he installed some gym equipment in the spare room and burned calories three times a week. Amaka started exercising too, but she wasn't keen on the routine. At first, it was fun sweating together in the same room, accompanied by loud music. But after a few weeks, she was content with being a spectator and blending smoothies for her action man. They had a washing machine in the bathroom of this spare room and piled dirty clothes in a basket for the end of week washing. Amaka did not like to air her underwear under direct sunlight, so she started spreading them on the handlebar of the treadmill or stationary bicycle.

'But you've never said anything about it,' Amaka responded.

'Because I haven't said anything doesn't make it right, does it?'

Ehigie propped himself up on one elbow and looked his wife straight in the face.

'I don't see how you can complain about me hanging shirts on the wardrobe door or the back of the chair when you are guilty of hanging your pants on my bike.'

During their courtship, Ehigie had said Amaka suffered from Obsessive Compulsive Disorder. She had laughed it off saying

OCD was a white man's disease. Those times, she would come to his apartment and clean the entire house, make his bed and even fold his clothes in his drawers. She always arranged his boxers and t-shirts in the top drawer according to colour. His trousers would be put on one side in the second drawer and his shirts on the other side. She had a separate drawer for his socks and another for his bottles of perfume and deodorant. She also spent hours in the kitchen. He didn't like it when she washed plates he had already washed and put on the rack, but she said there was a difference between washing with liquid soap and a bar soap. He economised by using soap slivers from the bathroom to wash plates in the kitchen; she believed that it was unhygienic and that plates needed their own proper bath. After she cleaned the house, she would deliberately leave a piece of her clothing in his wardrobe. Ehigie had thought it funny that she marked territory this way, like lions or dogs did when they peed.

'Since we are beating out our little demons, could you please stop leaving piss for me to sit on in the toilet,' Amaka said softly. 'A gentleman is supposed to lift the toilet lid and seat before spraying, and then, when he is done, drop the lid and flush.'

'I never said I was a gentleman. Or did I ever say a gentleman was toasting you? You saw me and accepted me, so why do you want me to be gentle now? Have you seen a gentle Edo hustler?' Ehigie was now sitting on the chair. 'I don't even see why you have to flush the toilet after peeing; it's just a waste of water,' he added.

'Ehn! With that your toxic alcoholic urine? I can't have that stink in the same room with me o.' Amaka crossed her legs and turned away from him. Ehigie was tired and didn't want to continue the conversation, but he decided to throw in the towel after one last punch.

'Since you are so prim and proper, I decided to test how good you are with smells, but you failed the test. I put your toothbrush into the toilet and flushed, and then I put the brush back in your toothbrush case. You couldn't tell if it was clean or dirty because I saw you use it this morning. I am off to bed. See ya.'

Amaka could not believe what he just said. She screamed and jumped on his back, hitting him with the palm of her hands. Ehigie held her by both thighs and turned it into a pony ride. 'You know I am just kidding. How could I ever do that?' He galloped with her into the room and put her on the bed.

Because of Amaka's constant complaints, Ehigie decided to change. So, when he woke in the night to relieve himself, he chose to pee in the bathtub. He didn't want the sound of rushing water to wake Amaka, so he didn't run water into the bathtub. This turned out to be a terrible decision. When Amaka noticed yellowish pee in her bathtub the next morning, she gave Ehigie a lengthy tongue lashing. Ehigie decided to start peeing outside the house. He found a spot between the dog house and the fence; he called it wetting the flowers. When Amaka noticed, she laughed, but Ehigie didn't stop.

Late April, and the rains had not come. It had become worrisome for farmers and everyone because of the fierce heat. The issue of global warming suddenly took on renewed significance. The well behind the house had dried up, but Ehigie and Amaka did not know immediately. They had taken the house because the caretaker showed them water running from the kitchen tap and told them there was a borehole in the backyard. It was only after they had moved in that they discovered that the borehole was only a well, nine metres deep.

The morning they discovered the dried-up well was a bad one. Ehigie and Amaka were used to turning on the submersible pump whenever the overhead tank was empty. So, there was no need to store water in big drums in the house. That morning, Ehigie woke up early to have his bath and unusually flushed before deciding he had to do a poo. While he was on the toilet seat, he let his hot water run into a bucket for his bath. He tried to flush afterwards, but there was no water in the cistern. He thought he would just turn on the pump after his bath. He got dressed and went out to turn on the pump, but there was no water. His plumber could fix a burnt pump, so Ehigie called and was lucky that the plumber was in the neighbourhood. When the plumber got to the house, he checked the well and gave Ehigie the good news first. Nothing was wrong with the pump. Then, the not-so-good news: the well had dried up.

Back inside the house, Amaka had woken up and wanted to get ready for work. She walked into the bathroom and opened the toilet lid. Fireworks like the fourth of July erupted in her head. Ehigie quickly explained what had happened and asked the plumber to reveal his findings. Ehigie excused himself and left for work when Amaka would neither listen nor be pacified. Amaka had to get packs of sachet water – everyone called it pure water – to have her bath and flush the toilet.

That morning, Amaka arrived at her office late, fuming at all the times she had sat on her husband's pee. Titus, her office assistant, was at his desk when she got in. She called him into her office and asked for a report she had asked him to prepare for a meeting. Titus apologised and said it wasn't ready; he promised to get it ready before lunch break that same day. Amaka nodded and watched him leave. She powered up her laptop and typed a letter terminating his appointment. Thirty minutes later, she called Titus into her office and handed him the letter. Titus broke down in tears. He went on his knees and pleaded, but his boss didn't budge. Amaka quietly asked him to hand over his I.D card and leave her office. He had thirty minutes to clear his desk and leave the premises.

Titus cleared his desk slowly, sniffing. His colleagues knew better than asking questions openly. They acted like nothing was happening, but their phones were very much alive: text messages zipped through cyberspace, announcing themselves as barely audible WhatsApp notifications: two ticks for the sender, a ping for the receiver.

> Isaac: *O boy wetin de happun?*
> Chucks: *E be like say Madam craze don start. All man take cover. B like say Tito de peal out.*
> Isaac: *Tito commit abi? Wetin e do?*
> Chucks: *Bros, how I wan take know?*
> Isaac: *I go block Tito for outside. If madam ask, tell am say I go buy water for office.*
> Chuks: *K. But no tay o.*

Titus was a shattered man. He sat on the landing outside the office, held his head and cried. He could not believe what had just happened to him. He was sure the report wasn't needed that day because it was meant for a business meeting he had scheduled personally for the coming week. He thought of his children. They were on holidays and would resume school in three weeks. The school management had, at the end of session party, notified parents of an increase in school fees the following session. Titus now had to pay over two hundred thousand naira for his three kids. His monthly salary was a little below one hundred thousand, after tax. Now, even that inadequate income was gone. His wife ran a petty trade but was now at home as advised by the doctor. She was pregnant with baby number four and counting down to her EDD. Titus left the office complex and decided to walk home. As he walked, he saw a bar and went in. When he opened his first bottle of beer, he sent Amaka a text message: *Please ma, I am very sorry for what I did. I will never play with my work again. May God touch your heart ma.* He waited for a reply and kept looking at the screen hoping the reply would come. He sipped the fifth bottle still hoping for a reply so that he would not have to go home to tell his wife that he didn't have a job.

Amaka closed from work early that day and went shopping. She bought five fifty-litre kegs to fetch water with from a bank near the supermarket. She tipped the security guard to help her fill her containers. Through the following weeks, Amaka rotated fetching water from three different places so that people would not get tired of her and stop her from fetching. She discovered that it was a lot cheaper to fetch water herself than buy from boys who pushed gallons of water in specially fabricated carts. Most of the carts had graffiti on them: *Water show boy. He who bring wota bring life. Overflowing water. My cup neva run dry. Water his live.* It was like a criterion to have something written on the cart, no matter the spelling or language. A twenty-litre gallon sold for three hundred naira, and the boys were highly sought after. They would say 'oga don buy am all,' even when they weren't completely sold out so that one would raise the offer. Amaka's neighbour bought a cheap phone for one of the water boys so that whenever she called, he would wheel water to her house. It worked the first day; the next day when she called, the caller prompt said the number did not exist on the network.

Ehigie saw this water fetching business as tasking for his wife and decided to take it up. On his first day, he took the kegs in his car but had a business meeting that went on late into the night. That day, Amaka had to buy four packs of pure water to have her evening bath and cook dinner. After that episode, she thanked Ehigie every time he offered help, but always got the water herself.

With the continued water scarcity, the duo took decisions on water consumption. The first was that they didn't have to flush the toilet if it was only peed in. Second, they decided to always use the toilet without flushing it before taking a bath. They would then block the bathtub drain while they had their bath and afterwards scoop the water into a bucket and use it to flush the toilet. Amaka was embarrassed the first time she saw her husband do this honourably. Ehigie noticed his wife's reluctance to conserve and recycle water this way and reminded her of their University days.

'I can't remember a day in all my life at the university hostel when I used the toilet. As early as 4 am, you will see light from a hundred different flashlights searching for the perfect spot to excrete in the bush. Guys, especially, had conditioned themselves to always go in the morning so that they didn't have to go during the day, no matter the quantity of beans they ate. The girls usually did what they called 'shot-put.' They would do their business in the comfort of their rooms in a polythene bag and fling the bag through the window. Some would carry the bag to a nearby garbage dump and toss it. They would then spray the room with air freshener or perfume. There was this day a girl tried it and got a terrible result. As she tossed the bag through her window, the bag hit the burglary proof bars and didn't get the required distance. The contents of the bag spilled and rolled down the wall. She was on the third floor of the hostel. So, the thing slid down her window, down the window below her and that of the room on the ground floor. The smell from the bag was deadly. That day all the girls on the block decided to trace the source of the smell. They waited till it got very dark, and around 11 pm that night they banged heavily on Fatima's door. She could hear the angry voices outside her room and broke down in tears. She promised to clean up the entire building the next day if they spared her. They did. So, she called her father and told him the story and he sent a cleaning agency to the hostel the next day to clean the entire place, especially the toilets.'

Two weeks into their water preservation initiative, Amaka was getting ready to leave for her office when she noticed a motorcycle parked in front of her house. Who would come visiting early in the morning? She wondered. She had told the gateman several times to stop receiving visitors at his duty post. She walked outside to see who it was and recognised Titus sitting on a concrete slab over the drainage. Titus had come to her house with his pregnant wife and children. She wondered how all of them had fit on the motorcycle; they must have looked like something out of a circus. Immediately they saw her approach, the entire family prostrated in front of her. They refused to get up, even when she insisted that they should. 'Abeg ma, abeg ma.' The family said repeatedly. Even the smallest child, whom Amaka guessed was between two and three years old, joined in the chorus. 'Abeg ma. Abeg ma. Abeg ma…' The heavily pregnant woman was uncomfortable in her position. She looked stuck in the middle of a press-up. The sight sickened Amaka. Had she become a monster? Ehigie was at the back of the house making sure both their cars had engine oil and water in their radiators. He had been busy and had not checked the cars over the weekend as was his weekly routine. Satisfied with the cars, he hopped into his and drove towards the gate. He saw people prostrating in front of his wife and wondered what on earth was going on. He recognised Titus and figured it was an office matter. Ehigie did not stop or look at his wife as he drove past them. Amaka knew her husband well enough to know that there was going to be a row later. He should have stopped to ask what the matter was or something, but he didn't. She knew he had concluded that she was the problem.

True to her thoughts, Ehigie came home that night sniffing for blood. She did not wait for him to pick on her, she confronted him as he went into the bedroom to change his clothes.

'So, what is it this time around? What crime have I committed?' she asked.

'Oh, so you are now a demigod that people prostrate to abi? All Hail Amaka. That's how you want to treat everybody around you? Well, not in this house. I won't have it; don't even begin to think you can tell me what to do in my own house.'

Ehigie's voice had a strange quality to it. It was totally devoid of humour, and in its place, Amaka discerned the capacity for great damage and violence. She had merely wanted to have the upper hand by confronting her husband first, but she now saw that it was a bad idea. 'Nor be person wey first call police dey win case,' she thought. Ehigie marched into their bedroom and took off his shirt and singlet. Amaka could see his bulging muscles. 'This man will kill me if I aggravate him,' she thought. An image of Ultimate Warrior flashed through her mind. When the wrestler had taken a beating and was ready to turn the bout around, he would hold unto the ropes around the ring and prop himself up. Any blow thrown at him would not matter as he would conjure strength from mystical sources. After that, he would give his opponent a beating that was both painful and spectacular to watch.

'Why didn't you stop to find out what was going on?' Amaka asked a bit less violently. 'If those people came to kill me in your house that's how you will let them kill me, abi? I am not safe in your house o. I am going!' She turned and walked briskly toward the living room front door. As she walked, she hit her shin against a side stool. She groaned, stumbled and fell. She got up and paused at the front door fiddling with the key in the lock. Ehigie ran after her but stopped when he saw her hobble to the door.

'Are you not a demigod?' the anger had gone out of his voice and left a taunt behind, 'why can't you just fly through the keyhole?'

'Leave me alone o, you wife beater.'

'Did I touch you? Fear-fear woman.'

'Go away! Leave me alone. I will call my father for you.'

Ehigie soon lost the taunt and calmed down.

'So why were Titus and all those people prostrating to you this morning?'

'He came with his family to beg for his job after I fired him.'

'You fired Titus? Why? That man is your longest serving staff. You made him resign from his former job to work with you, and now you fire him? Please give the poor man back his job, before his village chief comes to draw chalk lines across my gate.'

Amaka stood by the door nursing her leg.

'It was all your fault! You made me sit on your smelly pee! Why do you always pee on the toilet seat?'

Ehigie sat on the stool that almost amputated Amaka's leg. He wondered why this toilet affair mattered so much; why he couldn't do what he wanted in his own house.

END

AKIN

Akin stared, unbelieving, at his wife's phone. He had woken to the shrill sound of his wife's alarm. She was in the bathroom getting ready for another day at the national theatre when the alarm went off. Akin had reached out to stop it but decided to check the time. What he saw on the screen took the sleep from his eyes. It was a reminder; it read: *Birth C. Implant.*

Akin and Aisha had been married for three years: three years of bliss and happiness, only sometimes dampened by the wait for a child. As Akin stared at the screen of his wife's phone, he wondered what his wife wanted with a birth control implant. Was she having one removed or fitted? Why hadn't he known about it? He was a doctor and really loved children. He couldn't wait to have his own bundles of joy.

In the three years that Akin had been married, his cousins and members of his family had badgered him to have children or take another wife. Everyone bothered Akin, except his mother. His mother had told him her story, of how even though she had had four daughters, Chief's people would not let her rest until she birthed a son – Akin.

Akin said nothing to his wife that morning. Rather, he resolved to ask one of his friends, an expert on fertility issues, what his wife could want with a birth control implant.

Akin was the only son of the Omotoshos. His birth was the gas that rekindled the flame of hope and kinship within the family. Between twelve years and four girls, terrible gossip and suspicion had widened the gulf between Akin's mother and Chief's family. There were heated verbal attacks and general impatience in the family, especially when relatives were around. Being the family head, Chief Omotosho barred his sisters from coming to his house to embarrass his wife. Rumour had it that Akin's mother had been in a group during her university days where girls exchanged their unborn male children for marriages to super-wealthy men. Another story said she was from a lineage of witches who all suffered the same fate. Mrs Omotosho was bothered by all the venomous gossip, but she had also read enough to know that it was the man who determined a baby's gender: she simply nurtured in her womb, what she had been given. But outwardly, she had the simple reticence that children and their gender were God's prerogative. Eventually, Akin came, and his mother was the happiest woman on earth.

The Omotoshos had intended to raise Akin as they raised his sisters, but they pampered and protected him. Akin had everything from the most expensive gadgets to the most recent cartoons. The Omotosho's house was always lively and filled with Akin's friends. Akin was an average student and scaled through primary and secondary school without difficulty. He was later admitted to study medicine at the University of Lagos. The day his admission letter came, Akin's father stretched clenched fists, telling his boy to tap one. Akin first pointed to the left but stopped, mumbled some incoherent mumbo jumbo, scratched his head in thought and tapped his dad's right fist. Both fists had car keys in them, what type of car was the surprise. Akin was every bit glad about his choice. He had picked a sleek black Mercedes over a hatch-back Honda model.

Medical school was not easy; what with the inadequate facilities and the ever-striking lecturers? Mrs Omotosho could not understand why her boy wasn't sent abroad in the first place. After all, two of her daughters were comfortable in the United Kingdom. Akin was the heir, why did he have to go to a Nigerian university?

'This boy has to know where he comes from to get to the top,' Chief Omotosho had said. The 'Akin go or stay' debate was now by the way. Frontiers Specialist Hospital, Victoria Island had become a name that cut across Nigeria and drew patients from other African countries. With his money and connections, Chief Omotosho was able to set up a hospital for his son with state-of-the-art equipment flown in from Germany. The place was 'it'. Children would even fake a tooth ache just to visit the giant molar shaped section where they were allowed to man one of the numerous video game consoles as they waited to see a dentist. Kids always left with a complimentary toothbrush.

According to Akin's friends, Akin was large and in charge. Most of his friends wished him well while some were green with envy. His female friends fought tooth and nail – some physically tearing off their glued-on nails and wigs – to win his affection in his bachelor days. His father had nudged him with the saying that when a child is old enough to carry a hoe, he gets a hoe. So Akin had to make a choice among the women who trailed him like the Pied Piper. That was how Akin came to be with Bunmi.

Bunmi and Akin had been going steady for over a year and Mrs Adelaja, Bunmi's mother, had started to see a future in high-brow gatherings and on the cover of glossy magazines with Akin as her genie. How to rub the lantern was her problem; then she came up with a plan.

'Look, Bunmi, your father's health is deteriorating, and you still have five younger ones waiting to go to university.'

Mrs Adelaja softly broke the scheme to her daughter one evening, holding the girl close to her and stroking her long hair; the plan was neither novel nor ingenious.

'My daughter,' she said, 'you have always lived up to expectation; taking responsibility when you need to. In this case...' she paused.

'Yes Mummy,' Bunmi said, turning to look at her mother.

'All you need to do is get pregnant for this boy so that he will marry you.'

Bunmi was stung! 'What? You want me to trick Akin into marrying me?' Bunmi paused briefly but her mother did not respond. 'This is so painful. It means you think I am already sleeping with him. That's even beside the point. If that poor boy is going to marry me, then let him do it because he wants to. I couldn't live with myself knowing that I forced a man to marry me. I won't do it mum, I won't.'

Mrs Adelaja kept quiet, cocked her head at an odd angle and simply looked her daughter in the face. Gradually the wisdom in her words distilled and Bunmi seemed to understand. She would do it. She really liked Akin and wanted to keep him.

'But Mum, what if he doesn't marry me? This is a trick. What if he knows I am tricking him?'

'Hey, there is no trick there; this is not juju. Will you make yourself pregnant? He will marry you, just get pregnant and leave the rest to me.'

Akin was always mostly content with just spending time with Bunmi and having a conversation. It seemed like he had been warned or something, so he didn't touch Bunmi. Bunmi took this little problem to her mother. The old woman looked at her child in silence for a minute then broke into a loud guffaw, tears rolling down her cheeks. The woman cooed devilishly, holding her head.

'Get out of my sight! You little cricket. Oh, so you want me to bear children for you abi? With all the *iyanga* you and your mates do in school with all those tight trousers and "show me your back". You mean to tell me you don't know what to do?'

Mrs Adelaja pulled herself together, wiping her tears with the end of her wrapper.

'Listen to me...'

Bunmi made reservations at a resort. The offer of a getaway from the office was out of this world, and Akin jumped at it. The weekend came and passed, and Bunmi's mother raided her with questions; not giving the girl the chance to answer any. Bunmi told her mother that everything was under control just to get her mother off her back.

One night, Akin dropped Bunmi off at her parents' after a dinner date. He turned off his headlights and just basked in her presence in the car. Akin had given Bunmi a ring that evening. He was not one for public displays of affection, but he had said he wanted her and was willing to spend the rest of his life with her. She had accepted. Bunmi got down from the car and was going in when her mother bounded out, head tie around her waist and stood in front of Akin's car.

'Come down, young man,' she said

Akin came down and bowed good-naturedly. 'Good evening ma,' he greeted.

'Good evening. Did my daughter tell you?'

Akin was lost. He looked to Bunmi for an explanation, but she too seemed lost.

'Mummy, I don't understand. She did not tell me anything.'

'Oh, she did not tell you that she is pregnant, abi? Well, she is pregnant.' The woman went into overdrive. She did not notice the shock on Bunmi's face or the bewilderment of Akin's face. She rattled on. 'You will not know; you cannot know. When you were busy despoiling my daughter, you did not know. Now she is pregnant; you are saying she did not tell you. Look, in this family, we do not abort babies, and my grandchild cannot be a bastard. In fact, you can't put my daughter and me to shame. So, quickly go and bring your people and come and do the right thing before she starts showing…'

'Mummy,' Bunmi said.

'Will you shut up? What are you mummying me for? Didn't you go with him that weekend? Oh, you think I didn't know?'

'Mummy I'm not pregnant,' Bunmi said.

'Ehn? I thought you said everything was under control?' Mrs Adelaja faced her daughter. 'You disgraceful child, but…'

Akin got into his car and zoomed off. Bunmi burst into tears, shoved her mother aside and ran into the house.

Four years had passed since Akin stormed out of Bunmi's life and whooshed into Aisha's. Earlier in their marriage, Akin had visited a hospital to get himself checked after his wife didn't conceive in their first year. The doctors pronounced him normal. He had then suggested that Aisha went for a check-up. She had been furious and accused him of being barbaric and told him never to bring up the issue. She asked him if he was questioning God. However, some weeks after the argument, she relented, and they both went to a gynaecologist who examined her and pronounced her normal as well. The gynaecologist had made known that their predicament was common with newlyweds and that they should relax and give it time.

When Aisha came home that evening, on the day Akin saw the birth control reminder, Akin offered to help her out of her clothes. He grabbed her tenderly from behind as she stood in front of her wardrobe. He gently peeled off her blouse, kissed her neck and nibbled on her earlobe. Aisha closed her eyes and enjoyed the feeling as her husband removed her clothes. Akin lifted her blouse over her head but did not pull it over her arms, so both her arms were in the air while her blouse covered her head. He then touched her left arm bicep and felt a tiny lump. It had to be the birth control implant where his friend had said it would be. Aisha froze. She slowly removed her blouse by herself, still in her husband's embrace. She looked in the mirror in front of her and she could see the tears rolling down Akin's face.

'How could you do this to us?' he whispered in her ear, tightening his hold on her. She burst into tears as well. He didn't let go of her as he felt her body go limp. He took a step closer to the drawer where she could lean on and support her weight.

'I didn't think you would understand,' she muttered.

'Understand what?' Akin asked. He guided her to the bed and they both sat on the edge. She told him how his career was flourishing and how she also wanted a flourishing career too. She didn't want pregnancy or child bearing to ruin her chances of making it to the top of her career. She was a dancer with the state troupe and had travelled abroad for several performances. She had started a second degree and was hoping to qualify as a consultant on Creative Arts and Culture. Akin understood perfectly what his wife was saying, but he could not stomach why she took the decision on her own. If she had told him about her aspirations, he would have supported her, and they would have sought ways to balance child bearing with her career. He thought of the contacts he had and how easy it would have been to get his wife going, but what she did and how she did it amounted to a brutal betrayal.

Akin moved out of his house to his parents' home that night.

Michael Owen was everywhere on the pitch. With his pace, no one could stop him. His daring runs were a nightmare to any defender. Chief Omotosho chuckled in his expansive sitting room when Owen scored a fantastic goal, totally humiliating both the defender and the goal-keeper. The only glow in the house was from the TV set and Chief Omotosho sat in front of his giant screen, watching highlights of the English Premier League. It was 11 pm and past his bed time, but he refilled his bowl of gruel for the third time. Outside, Akin parked his car and came into the house.

'Ah! Daddy, Good evening sir.

'Welcome Akin.

'Daddy, what's happening? You are usually asleep at this hour. Is it the football...?'

'No, Akin. I was waiting for you.'

'Is there a problem? Akin showed concern.

'Akin, there is no problem. Go and eat, then we can talk.'

'It's already late sir; I'll just go in and change.'

Fifteen minutes later, Akin returned and sat on a chair close to his father.

'How was work today?' the old man began.

'Fine sir, the usual routine. Erm...Daddy, what is it you want to see me about?'

'Akin, your mother and I have been wondering what the matter is. Especially the way you carry yourself these days.

'How do you mean, sir?'

'Please be patient; don't rush me.'

'I am sorry sir.'

The old man croaked on; he picked up the remote control to reduce the volume of the set but turned it off altogether. The room was plunged into soft darkness; a warm glow seeped in from the security lights outside. Chief Omotosho put a hand on Akin's knee.

'Akin, your hospital is doing well. We are all happy. Everybody holds you in high esteem. But you go around with this defeated attitude. Your mother and I know something is wrong. And now, you have decided to come to stay with us. You are a man, and I am sure you can carry your own burdens. But, Akin, this is my house; and you are still my son.'

'Daddy...,' Akin started, but paused.

'Yes Akin, what is the matter?'

'Daddy, every day I see people with different sorts of problems and difficulties. Day in, day out...'

'So, you want to kill yourself? You're already doing what you can to help those people. You cannot drink *Agbo* for another man's *Jedijedi*.'

'Daddy, I honestly don't know how to say what I want to say now. That woman in my house wants to kill me.'

'God forbid! How can you say that about your wife?'

Akin told his father about the birth control implant he had discovered.

Chief Omotosho found Akin's story shocking, but he received it calmly. He thought about how Akin's mother had travelled to church programmes in different states with the same prayer point. The woman was currently on one of such prayer trips where she went to pray for a child for her only son. She blamed herself for his situation because she thought it was hereditary, forgetting her scientific empiricism. She had fasted for many days and nights in the past three years. She had lost weight and did not bother much about her appearance. No matter how many times chief persuaded her to stay home, Akin's mother insisted that she was one more visit away from the man of God who would miraculously help her son. She had even been in an accident but escaped without hurt. But that was not enough to deter her. Chief Omotosho sighed and told Akin to be very careful with his wife.

'My son, I think your wife has done this because she wants to be reckless on her road shows. It is safer for her that way, can't you see it? You should know how artistes behave? You of all people know why celebrity marriages don't last. It's because they want to behave as if they are single, while married.'

Akin didn't think so, but he knew his father had a point. Chief Omotosho then suggested that his son get a divorce immediately. The family lawyer could start the paper work as soon as possible. Both men were silent, in thought, until they both fell asleep on the living room sofa.

Akin never took a decision when he was angry. Time, he knew, always put things in perspective. He loved his wife, but he felt used for three years. He wondered why it was the people one loved were capable of hurting one the most. How could his wife, his best friend, do this? He felt his life falling around him. One evening, as he watched a documentary about starvation and death, he saw himself as one of the big-headed, pot-bellied and malnourished kids waiting to be pecked by one of the hovering vultures. He then decided to go out and help those who were less privileged. He gathered a team of his friends and proceeded on a one-month medical expedition to Northern Nigeria.

Steaming coffee, emerald green lights, black marble counter. Akin sat with his feet barely touching the black marble floor. A week after his return from his month-long medical outreach, Akin found himself in the coffee parlour and bar all by himself; not speaking, eating little, bearded like a forest and drowning in thoughts stimulated by the aroma and taste of hot coffee. It was getting late and he had to go home. He felt a little hungry and knew it was a good sign. He got up from his seat and remembered that he had not turned on his phone since he came back. For Akin and his colleagues, their phones had been useless during their expedition because there was no coverage in the towns they visited. When Akin turned his phone on, countless messages flooded in, and he decided to read them. Only then, did it hit him how long he had been cut off. After reading the messages, Akin got up, left the coffee bar and hopped on a bus.

On the bus, Akin sat with his eyes closed, trying to shut out all the noise. He got off two bus stops shy and walked the little distance to his father's house. The house was unusually crowded. The house had been that way since Akin returned from his expedition and news of his return blessed the family. Somehow, news of the 'evil wife' had leaked and salt and pepper had been added to the story.

Akin felt the piercing gaze of his family as he walked into the compound and into the kitchen where he predicted his mother would be. He held her and kissed her on the cheek softly. He whispered into her ear how much he had missed her and how guilty he had felt all along for abandoning his wife. He told his mother he wanted to forgive Aisha. He had made a vow before God to stick with her in good and bad times. These, he said, were bad times occasioned by his wife's bad decision, and he was going to stand by her. Since he now knew the source of the problem, the solution would surface. Akin's mother hugged him and whispered in his ears that he should go.

Akin's fingers trembled as he turned the keys in the lock to his house. He held his breath as he slowly pushed the door open and his head caught a spider web as he stepped into the house. He knew Aisha wouldn't be in the house, but he needed to get there. He walked through the house like a zombie, into the lifeless kitchen and the adjoining store. Before things went mad, the kitchen always had the smell of some delicacy. With time, Akin had come to associate the aroma of food from the kitchen with home. Leaving the kitchen, he walked to their bedroom and felt the emptiness. His wife's dressing table was empty, except for two bottles of perfume. The mirror, the same one that had borne witness to countless moments of joy and tenderness had gone dusty. Akin thought fleetingly that if he cleaned the dust, he might find happiness lurking within. But he also remembered that the last witness the mirror bore was the sight of him asking his wife why she stopped them from having children. The mirror had watched, or recorded, how he had walked out of their matrimonial home leaving his wife dejected and sorry.

Akin decided to leave the mirror alone.

He sat on the edge of the bed and was immediately irritated by the dust he unsettled. He coughed and sneezed vigorously, unsettling some more dust. He saw an envelope on the drawer and picked it up. As he picked up the envelope, he saw the clean rectangle underneath it and really had an idea of how much dust had gathered in the house. Akin did not open the envelope immediately. Even though he recognised his wife's writing.

Aisha was a very beautiful woman. Akin remembered watching her on stage when she performed at an open-air theatre in Jos. She totally transformed during her performance, evolving into the character she played, trance like. He knew from the first time he said 'Hi' to her that he loved her and would do anything to become significant in her life – perhaps, become her life's one constant.

For Akin and Aisha, the feeling was not mutual at the beginning. It had taken Akin to conscript a friend who knew Aisha to set up a date. It was a short date in Lagos and Akin had arranged Aisha's transportation from her house in Abuja down to his own house. Akin got a return Abuja – Lagos ticket and asked his friend to give it to Aisha. A cab driver got to her apartment as early as 6:30 am and drove her to the airport. She got on the flight and landed in Lagos to the waiting placard of another chauffeur who had her name written in red and pink ribbons; the driver had driven her to her breakfast date with Akin. Akin had made reservations at a restaurant with a sit-out on the fifth-floor balcony. The view from up there was nothing like she had ever seen. There were speed boats zipping past and larger, much slower vessels taking their time to glide over the Atlantic. Akin and Aisha ate and chatted; gone were Aisha's misgivings about going to see a man she barely knew. Gone was her anger at the man's temerity. After spending about two hours together, the chauffeur appeared to whisk Aisha back to the airport in time to catch her return flight.

Akin knew he was going to marry Aisha when he travelled to France to watch her perform at an African heritage concert. During her performance, she had seen him in the audience and fallen on stage because she had no idea he would be there. She got up and pretended that her fall was part of the act. She got a lot of cheers because the fall synchronised with the beats and heightened the effect of the slave plantation dance she was performing. He took her to Disneyland in Paris the next day as if his surprise appearance wasn't enough. It was there in Paris, in Disneyland, that Akin had made his intentions concrete. He did not want a casual, fleeting friendship. He wanted a lifetime.

It pained Akin to think that Aisha had decided to delay childbirth without his consent. But he was ready to forgive her and be happy again. They would move on and start a family; they would do everything to make sure that her career did not suffer because of childbirth. It would be difficult, but they would manage.

Akin was preoccupied with those thoughts when he tore open the envelope his wife had left him. He was afraid. What was it? A suicide note? Divorce papers, or a note asking him never to look for her? Could she have run far away? Suddenly, he lost the strength to know. Whatever was in the note, he would find out later. He backed against the wall and slid to the floor. It is a common saying that walls have ears. Did they have mouths too? These walls that had witnessed their love, his agony at the lack of a baby; what had they witnessed in his absence? Had his family members come to harass his wife? Had she cried and begged that she would change? Had she tried to contact him? He looked at the note, but he didn't pick it up. Whatever it was, he would find his wife. He picked a pen and started to scribble. Aisha needed to know that he too had suffered. Their marriage had reached a threshold and they would move beyond it. When he was done, he had a poem:

Insomnia.
I lie in bed, eyes shut tight.
'tis almost pitch black night,
Save for the incandescent glow from the moon
Squeezing through dark clouds.

Sleep dances round my eyes; taunting me.
So close I can feel her, yet so far, can't reach her.
Her calming hypnotic spell eluding me.

All is quiet save for chirping crickets and toads,
Each, calling for a mate tonight.
The last power plant goes out...
SILENCE.
Rapid Eye Movement. I blink with eyes shut.
Perhaps I can woo the caressing arms of slumber.

Mind darts...why?
Someone to speak to?
Am I the only one?
Toss 'n turn, curl; I'm worn - none works.

Now I hear the beat of my heart,
The throb as it pulsates life.

Heed oh fair one,
Soothe my weary eyes 'n cradle my heavy head.
Or are you too lonely and seek a companion;
One to watch with you tonight while earth sleeps?
Someone to count the stars with and to restore nature as she lays in
silent slumber?

Thou teaseth me, can I but heed this call...perhaps for a night,
My eyes shall see the dawning of new light with you.

END

WITHOUT YOU

Dareng died a few minutes after 2 am.

Simi sat quietly as the doctor checked for a pulse and a heartbeat. She watched as if in a trance as the doctor shook his head and the nurses covered Dareng with a white sheet and the doctor whispered that he was sorry. She was silent as the doctor spoke to the nurse: 'Time of death, 2:04 am.' It was when the doctor stepped out of the ward that something clicked in her head; she opened her mouth to scream, but no sound came.

Simi was dragged to a waiting room by two nurses who expressed their sympathies in kind, but professional tone. The medics were concerned because she wasn't wailing or rolling on the floor. She just sat, mouth open in a silent scream, obviously in shock. When the doctor asked for the number of a relative to call, Simi silently handed him her cell phone and whispered, 'Gyang.' Gyang was Dareng's younger brother who had come to holiday with them a few days before his elder brother was admitted to the hospital.

Simi and Dareng had been married for two years and were a very happy couple. They were soul mates. They did not have a child yet and did not see why they couldn't both enjoy life, trusting God for his blessings at the right time.

She had been the little girl next door when they were kids and their parents teased them both, calling them husband and wife. They had played House and cooked sand and hibiscus leaves in empty tomato cans behind the house. As they got older, the mention of Simi or Dareng would slap blushes on the other's cheeks. This soon grew into anger and rebellion: if one saw the other at a distance, he would go in the other direction. They stopped going to each other's house and refused to forgive anyone who teased them about marrying each other. But they soon shed all that childishness. They rekindled their love at the university and were inseparable. They got married soon after graduation.

When Gyang got the phone call about his brother's death, he was stunned. He started leaving for the hospital but stopped in the living room. Quickly, he went back into his late brother's room and went through the drawers. He brought out documents from various files and took their pictures with his camera phone. Gyang was particularly interested in the land sale agreements and rights of occupancy. Gyang called other members of the family to tell them of the unfortunate loss. He also dished out instructions to his siblings to go and get Dareng's car from the mechanic the next morning. They were to strip 'the barren witch who killed our brother' of everything. He brought down the flat screen TV on the wall and locked it in his room. He also grabbed a laptop resting on the dining table and locked it up as well. He looked around the house and was satisfied; he left for the hospital.

Later that morning, Gyang and his siblings scared out Dareng's ATM password from Simi. She could not believe that her husband's family had turned against her so quickly. These were people she had grown up with. Yet, they weren't giving her time to mourn her husband before the theft of her possessions began. She spoke to her mother on the phone, breaking the sad news to her and telling her of the events in her house. Her mum advised her not to object but just sit quietly and watch; she would be there soon.

Visitors started arriving around 3 pm, and the reality of Dareng's death became apparent. Simi was too sad and beat up to see any of her friends. She cried all day without eating. She refused to see visitors throughout that first day as she stayed huddled in her blanket. When she went out to urinate at night, she was touched to see some of her friends asleep in her living room. Some of them had spread some wrappers on the floor and used a cushion for a pillow; others simply rested their heads on their handbags.

Simi sat on the edge of the bed close to her mother and told her about some fights she had with Dareng. She liked to go to bed with the lights on while Dareng couldn't sleep without turning off the lights. Dareng had complained but she insisted on having the lights on. He had often stayed up late watching documentaries on Cable till she fell asleep before going into the room and turning off the lights. Once, he had mentioned it to a member of their support group in church and the man simply said, 'Brother Dareng, Satan is using your wife to challenge your authority. She is not submissive to you as the head of the house.' Dareng had been hurt and ashamed of letting anyone know about the little squabbles he had with his wife. He knew it would not be long before other members of the church would start whispering about how evil his wife was. He had realised that if he kept telling people what he did not like about his wife, they would form a bad opinion of her. That day, he got a custom-made sleeping mask with her name written boldly across it. She leaned over and kissed his blindfolded face the day she noticed it. He also told her that he felt stupid for letting his friend in on their little night fights. They had an understanding that night and it did not matter if the lights were on or off as they rekindled their feelings and hopes. When Simi fell asleep on her husband's chest, the lights were off.

When Simi finished this story, her mother held her and they both cried.

The wake was organised by members of their church who congregated outside the house and sat in rented plastic chairs. When friends and family started eulogising Dareng, Simi watched through teary eyes as Gyang lied. She wanted to get up and rain blows on the thief. Gyang was saying: 'I will do everything in my power to see that our wife is not left alone to suffer.' When Simi got up and walked into the house, people thought she was overcome by grief. Simi could not stand this hypocrisy. Gyang, the same Gyang who had acted as if a shaman had told him that his brother would die. The same Gyang who had held off grief until he and his brothers looted what they wanted in their brother's house. The same Gyang now promised to stand by her and make sure she was not left alone to suffer. Perhaps he fancied her. The idiot.

After the wake, Simi cried and coughed a lot. The coughing became uncontrollable and she began to feel feverish in a matter of minutes; her mother insisted she see a doctor. Sitting outside in chilly weather could have aggravated a cold. Fortunately, Simi had a doctor friend who quickly came around to check her. After inspecting her for a while, the doctor went to her car and came back with a pregnancy test kit. Simi and her mother looked at the doctor strangely.

The next morning, Simi woke up late but didn't care since she had nowhere to go. She saw the pregnancy kit on the drawer close to the bathroom door and decided to use it. While she was still sitting on the toilet bowl waiting for the test to reveal its findings, her mother knocked gently on the door saying Simi had a call. Simi opened the door and got the phone from her mum and at first, could not comprehend what her account officer was asking her. She and Dareng ran a joint account which her bankers knew of, and they were calling to find out if Simi had given her brother-in-law the power of attorney to change the mandate on the account to include him as a signatory. Simi declined the request and called on her mother to come and hear what she just heard. As she narrated the call to her mother, she started crying and dropped the strip on the toilet floor. When her mother picked it up, there were two bold red lines.

END

VERA THE VENUS FLYTRAP

I have a story about Vera my Venus flytrap to tell anybody who cares to listen. My name is Demola, and Vera is not a carnivorous plant sitting pretty and waiting to catch unsuspecting insects. She is human, feminine and goes after her victims; in this case, I am her ladybird.

Before we got married, Vera said she was pregnant. So, we had to get married quickly before she started showing; that way we would right our wrong in front of everyone. Wrong? What right had anyone to judge us? How could anyone call a child illegitimate when he had a consenting father and mother? Those are questions for another day. Let me just continue my story.

I didn't have a steady job at the time, so getting money for house rent was almost impossible. Somehow, I scaled that hurdle and rented a two-bedroom apartment. After that, I stared hopelessly at the bill from Vera's family: one hundred tubers of yam, two goats, one cow thigh for her parents, four boxes full of clothes and jewellery to be inspected by one of her aunties, five cartons of Beer, and three hundred thousand naira as dowry. I was to present these items to her family on the day of the traditional wedding. I was also supposed to put some money aside for her relatives who would come from the village. It was daunting, but I decided to take things one at a time. It was best to not worry about things, so I totally pretended like I did not know there was supposed to be a church wedding after the traditional. Left to me, there was nothing wrong with having the baby, and later in life when things were better, we could formalise our union. But no! Vera's parents would hear nothing of the sort. The irony of it all was that they did not give me a single naira for all their grandiose plans. I was in soup, and like my Lagos people would say when they wanted to offer understanding without help, 'I had entered one chance.'

It is often said that things become better after one gets married. So, I discerned that good things were enroute when I landed a job with a newspaper company. The company wanted someone who could speak Hausa to cover stories of insurgency in the North. I had learnt to speak Hausa at secondary school in Azare, Bauchi State; I was ready to do anything legal for cash, so I took the job. I also hoped that somehow, I would not be shot, maimed or blown to smithereens. The job paid very well and demanded that I travel often, which was very welcome at the time. After two weeks on the job, I asked my boss for a salary advance because of the wedding and he was gracious enough to tie me to a bond. I read the terms and conditions of the bond and quickly signed the documents. I saw that I was on an insurance policy because of the hazards involved in my kind of reportage. I thought my newspaper was really gracious.

I lost a lot of weight during the preparations for the wedding. I borrowed lots of money from colleagues who I had only just met. My old friends came through with their wonderful contributions: two crates of soft drinks here, a set of pots and pans there, and so on. Miraculously, again, I got a set of cane chairs for my living room. Vera wasn't working at the time, so she spent all her time and energy arranging the house and looking up wedding gowns and accessories on the internet. I wanted her to rent a wedding gown, but she would have no part of her big day borrowed. The joy was fully hers and no one – here she turned religious – except God, must take the glory. I had to pay for a customised gown.

Vera and her family invited ninety-five percent of our wedding guests. And for the MC, she wanted a comedian. 'My fee for the day is one hundred and fifty thousand naira,' the first comedian we approached said, distractedly. While we bargained his fees, he got a phone call from another intending couple and we heard him say, 'yeah…yeah, pay a commitment fee of sixty percent if you are serious.' My heart sank. We moved on and all the other promising MCs Vera suggested were overpriced. So, I had to call Okeoma, a classmate at university who made us laugh those days. He agreed to help me, for a small fee.

The day finally came and passed in a couple of hours. I was only able to pay Okeoma and the DJ from cash gifts guests tucked in my jacket pocket. When we got to our house, and I noticed that our gifts were not there. I asked Vera who informed me that they had been taken to her mother's place where they would be checked and prayed over before they were brought to us. When I asked how long it would take, she replied that she did not know. I didn't want to fuss, so I said nothing. But I wanted the gifts back because I intended to check them and sell some to recoup part of the money I spent on the wedding.

Once we got married, Vera started going through my phone, checking my photo gallery and text messages. I didn't mind at first because she was my wife; I assumed she would soon tire and realise that I was now her husband, not a boyfriend. In my playful moments, I sometimes thought about that word husband. It had a sense of going up -hus, and then coming down with a finality that bordered on permanence -band. It was more enforcing than boyfriend or fiancé. I wished Vera would think about it and stop checking my phone. She didn't.

One day, when I realised that Vera checked my browsing history and mail trails on social media, I objected. That was the day I realised that, as far as the matter was concerned, my choice had been taken away and replaced with obligation. 'If you don't have anything to hide, give me that phone now,' she said. I was angry, enraged really, but I could not touch her because of our baby. I looked at her and placed the phone on the table.

Our baby. Those early days of our marriage, Vera clung to me like I was the very air she breathed and fantasised about having a little me with all my facial features until she started craving abominable food combinations at odd hours. I agreed with Vera's every demand, especially when she became sluggish.

Vera complained bitterly about the pregnancy. She complained about almost everything she could see. When I asked, the doctor said the changes were hormonal, but it was simply crazy. She would not cook – the smell of oil and spices nauseated her. She was always tired – the baby was resting on her lungs; I wouldn't know, would I? She needed help around the house – didn't I see that her legs were swollen? I had to accede to getting a house help to do most of the chores in the house. So, Vera came home one day with this big boned timid girl who was to live and work in our house. Munirat, that was her name, came from a very poor background. The clothes she came in were threadbare; they told a story of extreme poverty and naivety. The colour was gone out of her clothes leaving only a shadow behind.

The skirt Munirat came in had been stitched in many places. The crude needlework announced themselves in incongruent colours. Vera gave Munirat some of her clothes and instructed her to take her bath twice a day. Vera looked for any excuse to throw her clothes at Munirat. 'This one has a stiff collar,' or 'something on this blouse itches my neck, I don't want a rash,' she would say.

Munirat amazed us. She told us she had finished secondary school and made good grades in her SSCE; she wanted to make some money to pay for JAMB exams so that she could go to university. On Munirat's first day, Vera had to show her how to wash plates with liquid soap. I imagined how this girl, who was out of secondary school and was coming to help Vera with house chores, could not do the littlest of things. But I wasn't bothered: Vera had brought her, and she would teach her. It was like listening to a broken record to hear Vera yell at the top of her voice repeatedly. Munirat could not spell Vaseline; she wrote 'visiline'. She spelled toothpaste as 'teethpast' on the shopping list Vera asked her to draw up. Yet this girl graduated from secondary school and with good grades too.

Since I did a lot of writing, and usually required silence, I decided to turn our spare room into a study so that I wouldn't disturb Vera every time I worked late into the night. That study was my sanctuary. I spent a lot of time there writing, drinking and having the occasional smoke. I was not a smoker, but I sometimes needed inspiration, and a bit of grass and some shots of brandy was always just right. Vera didn't complain; she had no power to do much else than sit around watching videos and commanding Munirat to do one more thing. When Vera came into the study, it was to watch me silently or to ask me for money for her ante-natal care. Gone was the 'you are the air I breath,' gone was she asking me how my day went. She was almost always irritable and tired.

Munirat slept in the dining area. When night fell, she would bring her mattress in from the sun and lay it out, while Vera and I retired. Somehow, Munirat started ironing clothes in my study. I shouted at her and told her to get out but she said it was 'Madam' who asked her to iron the clothes in my study. When I asked, Vera said she didn't want too much heat around her, and that she needed her space. Could I please not shout, it could affect the baby? And were they not my clothes that the girl was ironing? At first, I was upset. But gradually, I got used to it. I also found that I could ask Munirat to bring something across the table, so I didn't need to stand and break concentration.

It didn't take long for Munirat's 'rat' to surface. The rat started sneaking around the house, tying food in plastic bags and hiding them in the corners. After a while, the rat would take permission to visit her parents. Then the rat would do it all over again. We did not notice the rat at first. We just noticed that toothpaste, salt, sugar, seasoning cubes, milk, and other groceries were fast disappearing. Then I noticed that Vera was asking for food money too often. I was seething and waiting for an avenue to vent when one day I discovered a stash of food outside the house. I called Vera's attention to it and she told me not to worry. She asked for some money and bought a teddy bear which she placed at a strategic corner of the house. One day, Vera simply plucked out the eye of the teddy bear and plugged it into my computer. It showed Munirat stuffing foodstuff into plastic bags and putting them into the trash can. Vera gave the girl a heavy beating with the mop that day.

Usually, when Vera was at her nagging, I would sit it out in my study and simply drink some beer. Beer helped me work hard. Sometimes I fell asleep in the study, but Vera would come and drag me to bed. One day, I drank a little too much and I found myself at the Conseco Field house in Indianapolis. I was a featured artiste alongside Dr. Dre, Snoop Dogg, Ice Cube, Eminem and Nate Dogg. It was the 'Up in Smoke Tour' back in 2000. I stepped out of the 1964 Chevrolet impala 'six-four' on stage and the crowd went wild. We had the hydraulic system pumped, and the front tyre was suspended in the air. Four gold chains bobbed from left to right around my neck as I swaggered across the stage. I danced with a female fan on the stage grinding my hips against hers. My jeans were sagged and tucked in jet black Timberland boots. I spat lyrics for thirty minutes and rounded off my session by running to the edge of the stage to jump into the waiting hands of the crowd. That was when I saw Vera standing over me.

We had an unfortunate tragedy one day. It was early in the morning and Vera was screaming. She had pains and noticed blood on the sheets. I ran to our neighbour and begged him to give us a ride to the hospital. It wasn't easy carrying Vera into the car, but we did. I comforted her best I could, but she was in a special kind of pain. Her tears were one of anguish; I kept consoling her until the doctors took her away.

When the doctor came and asked me if I was a relative, I answered that I was her husband and knew the news was not good.

'Your wife is very fortunate to be alive, thank God. But I am sorry the baby didn't make it.'

I was numb for a few seconds. My neighbour and the doctor murmured their condolences. I thanked them and sat on the nearest chair I could find. When I gathered my thoughts, I asked the doctor why they didn't put the baby in an incubator. The doctor looked at me and smiled sadly.

'Take heart,' he put his hand on my shoulder, 'the foetus was young and had not developed enough to survive outside the womb.'

I looked at the doctor, what was he saying? 'But, Doctor, my wife was seven months gone, it should have…'

'No sir, your wife's pregnancy was barely three months old.'

I blinked. Vera and I had been married for about six months and she got pregnant before we got married. I thanked the doctor and stood.

'Please, take it easy,' the doctor said, 'I'm sure your wife can clarify all these when she is well enough.'

I thanked the doctor and made my way to Vera's ward.

I slept on a tiny bed in another room because the nurse said they didn't allow visitors sleep in the same room with their patients. The next morning, I waited for Vera to wake up. Once her eyes opened, I shot my question straight at her without a 'good morning'.

'How old was our baby?' Vera sluggishly turned and faced the wall. I got up and pulled her by the shoulder towards me. 'How old was our baby?' I repeated.

'Leave me alone,' she said. 'Can't you see I've just had a procedure?' I knew I wasn't going to get anything out of her that day, so I left the hospital.

I didn't go back to see Vera in the hospital, and honestly, I was not happy the day she walked into the house with her mother. I greeted her mother and nodded at her. From that day, I hardly came home early. I'd work my tail off at the office and when I got home, I would be tired and sleep immediately I hit the floor. Though Vera and I slept in the same room for her mother's sake, I slept on a duvet on the floor. We didn't talk or argue; all we had was silence: a bloated fragile silence, like a baloon waiting to be pricked.

One morning, two weeks later, Vera walked into my study and picked up the teddy bear on my table. The teddy bear, a box of perfume and a football jersey had been my birthday gift two months after our wedding. 'Wherever you are, whatever you do, just know I am watching over you, my angel,' she had said with a sweet smile when she placed the teddy bear on my table. I had accepted the teddy bear and other gifts as she smothered me with kisses. I had never moved the teddy bear.

I watched as Vera plucked out one eye of the teddy bear and removed what looked like a memory card. I was curious. She inserted the memory card into her tablet. She kept on swishing her finger on the tab till she stopped and burst into villainous laughter. She laughed so hard I was irritated. 'Can you get out of here?' I bellowed. She kept quiet and leaned into my face. I was seated in an arm chair and felt trapped. 'Look here Mr Man, if you don't want trouble, you will do exactly as I say.' She dropped the tab on my lap, and I saw myself there. Anxiously, I hit the triangle play icon and watched. I saw myself singing and dancing as if I was an artist at a concert; I was obviously very high. I rapped and mixed up the lyrics of P-Diddy, Snoop Dog and other artists. I was prancing on the chair like it was a car. Soon, I saw myself dragging Munirat and dancing after a feeble attempt at resisting. Soon, we were dancing a slow jam. When had this happened? I was still staring at the video dumbfounded when Vera picked up the tab.

'Now, Mr Man,' she said, 'you better start behaving yourself.'

I was stupefied. How could she equate smoking and drinking in my own house, and dancing with the housemaid with setting me up with a pregnancy? They were not the same. But I did not know how the Video ended. I had seen myself saying to Munirat, 'puff, puff, pass…' with a foolish smile and cough. I had seen Munirat sprawled in the crook of my arm. Then the singing and the slow jam with lights turned off like we were in junior high. Vera had taken the tab away before the video ended. What more was there?

My reality is sad. I didn't love Vera and had married her because she was pregnant. Now that she had miscarried, we are done. I begin to wonder why she even trapped me the way she did. She must have loved me or felt something for me to trick me so. She must have thought me a responsible person before making me her husband. But if she felt so strong about me, why did she punish me so much? Why was she so mean? I didn't have money, so that couldn't have been her motivation. Or was she just desperate to be somebody's wife? I don't understand it at all. But that is not even the issue. The real issue on my mind now is, 'how can I continue living with a woman I don't love?'

END

GUST OF EMERALD

It was a very formidable season. How on earth could they have found themselves in such a position? Waziri – Coach Waziri - died several times over during the match. Relegation was staring him in the face, and except something happened drastically, it would become his reality. The home crowd had gone mute, frozen in disbelief. It was the world on Garba's shoulders now. He had averaged twenty-two points per game since the season started with his strategy and amazing leadership as team captain. Today, all of that was about to become statistics for the book keepers. At the end of the third quarter, the Egrets were still losing at home to the Giants of Benue. Nothing worked out for the Egrets; their shooting from the free-throw line was deplorable, further narrowing their chances of an equaliser or a win.

A Giant wall around the trapezium prevented all Egret drive-ins and lay-ups; their only chance was to try for three-pointers. Waziri yelled for long range shots. Garba, playing with a hamstring injury, tried unleashing a series of shots to work some magic. But he seemed jinxed, as nothing worked. He then switched to holding the ball for long periods with remarkable dribbles, hoping to draw the attention of opposing defenders, and thereby create chances for his team-mates, but the Giants read the plan perfectly. It was a nightmare. The centre referee finally ended the match with the Giants going crazy with excitement over their seventeenth away victory.

Shame. Disbelief. Disaster. HORROR! The Egrets' wings had been clipped. All the players were silent in the dressing room. The usual game analysis and rundown were missing. The thought of playing in a lower division scared the melanin out of the players. They slowly packed their jerseys, stuffed their sneakers in rucksacks and walked away. Garba went home, disappointment edging him close to despair and depression.

Garba drove home, replaying the game plan in his head, with all the imagined style and glamour. During the last quarter, he should have been on fire, hitting clutch shots from all angles of the trapezium. The build-up from the back was well networked with big Jim finishing textbook style in breath-taking dunks or lay-ups. With little ease, the Egrets were skating on the in-door fibreglass court and running over the Giants.

Suddenly, Garba went painfully blind. The full beam of 'something' threw him into another realm. The deafening sounds of screeching tires and blaring horns were all too much for him to comprehend. Where did such heavy traffic spring from? Suspected burnt rubber filled the air, slowing his breathing, causing panic and a sudden rush of adrenalin. In a frantic effort to get away to safety, he followed his instincts, swerving the car wildly away from the unknown. Calm soon reigned, and Garba found himself on his serene street. The street was beautifully lit with orange streetlights. To his right, a couple walked along, engrossed in their evening fables, no traffic. This couldn't be. Garba pulled up to the curb and parked.

His heart was still in his mouth and his hands trembled nervously; he was drenched in cold sweat.

Somehow, Garba drove home and went straight to bed. Food had no appeal. Insomnia and some form of paranoia gripped him; the day's game still haunted him.

'If only my leg hadn't hurt so much, I would have been able to make a difference,' he mumbled. It was unusual for him to go into such self-pity and guilt, but it was also unusual to lose so badly. For the first time, Garba realised that one day he would no longer be able to participate in sports.

'How could I have been this stupid?' Garba said aloud. He had nursed the idea of channelling resources to importing cars and selling them back home but had not made any substantial move towards actualising this dream. The restless night was too much to bear. So, he rummaged through his chest of drawers and found some sleeping pills among some pain relievers. They didn't help. Thirty minutes later, he was as wide-eyed as an owl. His slight headache had become a full-blown migraine. Torture. Garba turned off the lights.

Garba hung morosely around the house for the next four days. He could not pull himself together. In four days, his usual clean-shaven head was mapped with kinky and unkempt hair. He had unusual signs of balding at a very early age and wondered where he got it from because neither his father nor grandfather was bald. Perhaps, it was a bad omen. He had not had a bath or eaten good food in four days. Time was of no relevance to him. Time for what? What did he have to do? Nothing!

Garba chased sleep around the house. He found it in the kitchen but couldn't hold onto it. He got a glimpse of it in the garage, but it simply vanished. Finally, as he lay exhausted face up on the dining table, the phone rang. It was like a clarion call. He had been in total isolation all this while. It had just been him alone in the same white clothes, surrounded by the same old soft white furniture. He reached for the phone and answered the call. The voice on the other end was the sweetest thing he had ever heard, or had he heard it before? He looked at the clock; it was exactly 10:24 pm.

Garba: Hello

Emerald: Hi. How are you doing?

Garba: Erm…I am fine and who am I speaking with?

Emerald: C'mon, don't tell me you don't recognise my voice.

Garba: Em. . . emm. Ooh! Of course, I recognise your voice. How was your trip? Guess you are now out of Port Harcourt.

Emerald: Fine, thanks, yes, I am out of Port-Harcourt.

Garba: Hope the girl's parents gave their consent or said something positive?

Emerald: Of course!

Garba: That's nice, they are getting married then. So, how are you generally?

Emerald: Very fine, thank you, and you?

[Silence.]

Garba: Why sound so British?

Emerald: Sorry.

Garba: For?

Emerald: Forgive me, Sire.

Garba: Very cynical. So, any more grown-up philosophy from you today?

Emerald: None yet.

Garba: Okay. Thank God. I don't know where a small girl like you got an old woman's brain from? I guess your grandma raised you.

Emerald: She's at home with me right now.

Garba: Thought as much.

Emerald: And my favourite, does that explain anything?

Garba: She's influenced you too much; guess you'd also learn values about the family and not pursue Condoleezza Rice's dreams.

Emerald: She is already downloading all that every day.

Garba: Good for you, learn from the best

Emerald: Guess you're back in Zaria, right?

Garba: Yup, and sulking.

Emerald: Haba! I thought we were through with that.

Garba: Nope. Your three minutes were just about average; I did not get enough consolation.

Emerald: Haba!

Garba: Just kidding. And where did you pick up "haba" from? I thought it was 'eehn!"

Emerald: I am now a "Samaru" in language, too.

Garba: No be beans.

Emerald: No, na yam.

Garba: Better yet. Na snail or periwinkle.

Emerald: Alright, your point has been made.

Garba: Which is?

Emerald: The periwinkle, snail point, enh.

Garba: I don't get it. What brought all that on, are you hungry? Bet you eat like crazy now and getting fat as well.

Emerald: Yes, I am getting really fat.

Garba: Na you sabi. But, do you add and shed weight at will? Because you change everytime I see you.

Emerald: Sort of, sometimes, not deliberately though.

Garba: Just don't add too much and lose all your "market value."

Emerald: You are something else.

Garba: Like?

Emerald: I am not for sale, so no fear of market value.

Garba: Haha. Says who?

Emerald: Me.

Garba: Ask your grandma?

Emerald: She, of course, will agree with me.

Garba: Nope. She'd tell you to rake in as much money as possible as dowry because you're a lawyer as well. Bet they'll discuss your net worth over some gin and partially roasted snails.

Emerald: No! No! No! Don't tempt me to say you're sick; I just may fall for it.

Garba: You just did.

Emerald: No, I did not!

Garba: Yes, you did. You're really stubborn and love quarrels in whatever form, pranks or otherwise.

Emerald: No, I don't! Not at all.

Garba: Yup, you do.

Emerald: On the contrary, I am a quiet little humble girl.

Garba: Tell that to the snails. A thief wouldn't come out in the open and declare he is one.

Neither would a humble little girl. Who told you, you are little? Old woman!

Emerald: Thank you.

Garba: For what?

Emerald: The compliment.

Garba: Which was?

Emerald: I like to think myself old.

Garba: Why?

Emerald: Nothing.

Garba: Bet that's why you give me such a hard time. There you go again.

You say something and say 'nothing.'

Emerald: Haba.

Garba: Naughty.

Emerald: I don't give you a hard time.

Garba: Yes, you do. First, you put me in quarantine, and then you get a restraining order limiting my visits to twice a year. What could happen next?

Emerald: I have to go.

Garba: See what I mean?

Emerald: I just got your birthday mail, thanks. I have a meeting that's why I have to go.

Garba: With the snail traders?

Emerald: I'll keep in touch.

Garba: Okay, if you say so.

Emerald: I say so, byeeeeeee!

Garba: All the best, then. Would have said "miss ya," but nahhh. It's the same, even when you are here.

Emerald: You are wicked!

Garba: No. But I do miss ya kind of. No, not kind of. Thought about you for some time but shook it off.

Emerald: Whatever, man. Bye.

Garba: You don't believe me?

Emerald: I said bye.

Garba: Okay. Whatever shape, you'd still look good. True talk.

Emerald: Thanks.

Garba: Now you can't even leave me with a lifeline, you are wicked.

Emerald: ALRIGHT.

Garba: Yeah.
Emerald: Take care of you, dear!!
Garba: I just might run onto the highway now.
Emerald: Please don't, bye.

Garba dropped the phone and was once again engulfed by that stinging disinfectant smell. The smell had ceased for a long while, and the room seemed to have been different just a moment earlier. He sat down and tried to recall the conversation he had just had, and with whom he had just spoken. He slowly looked around, and then slumped on the floor. Garba slept.

Two weeks later, at exactly 10:30 pm, Baba withdrew from the window where he had just watched Garba hang up the phone and go to sleep. Baba turned around, away from his subject. The old man slowly walked towards his apprentice who stood at the far end of the hall. Questioning eyes trailed his every step, but all were too afraid to speak. Garba's mother looked the most horrified of the lot. She had not eaten in days. She had boarded the first available flight from Lagos to Kano, and then she took a bus ride to Zaria. Baba stroked the beads around his neck, speaking softly to each one. By this time, his apprentice was on the floor, pounding leaves in a small mortar with his legs forming an X. Baba carefully scooped out the dark green paste and mixed it with some liquid. It was at this point that he spoke for the first time.

'You say na so your pikin dey do ev'ryday? E go talk, come lie down for ground?'

Garba's mother was taken aback by her sudden cue to participate. She attempted a reply but couldn't. She ended up nodding her head in agreement. With this information, Baba smoothened out the paste on a wooden board and stuck four shells in it. He froze. Looking sternly at the board, he bit his lips. After five minutes of silence, Garba's mother was flushed with renewed anxiety and thought more information would be relevant.

'Baba, after Garba talks about different things to his hand, that is the only time he can sleep,' she said.

Garba: What's your perspective on the different phases of your life: childhood, adolescence, youth, and adulthood? Hahahahah!

Emerald: I think life is an arc. You begin from the depths of innocence and finish at the depths of experience.

Garba: That's crap…it's like you're on Straight Talk Africa or something.

Emerald: So, what's your point?

Garba: Nothing. Okay, sincerely, why don't you have anything when I take you out?

Emerald: Could you rephrase that, please?

Garba: I mean, why don't you eat anything?

Emerald; Oh! I am always on a fast.

Garba: For what deity? More like cruelty, or for what cause?

Emerald: First, it's to God. Then, there is always one reason or another.

Garba: But does it exclude water?

Emerald: Depending on the individual.

Garba: Say what! How does the individual come in?

Emerald: And if you are doing forty days like I was the last time I saw you, you'll take water. So, I guess this brings us to the end of phase 1. Phase 2 will be on you.

Garba: What do you mean?

Emerald: I mean I'll ask all the questions next time.

Garba: What is phase 2? And what was 1?

Emerald: 1 was all of your questions, 2 will be mine!!

Garba: Shoot.

Emerald: Some other day, please. You are all too ready now.

Baba finally gets up and spits, not minding the freshly painted walls. He pulls out the phlegm from his lungs and "pptaaw!" He stands 1.7 metres tall and does something unthinkable. He unties his wrapper, which is knotted above his left shoulder. As the cloth drops to the ground, he raises both hands, staff in the right and beads in the left. Baba stands with his head raised to heaven, chanting. Garba's mother and her relatives all bow their heads, avoiding the sight of Baba's bare scalded buttocks in respect, shame, shock, disbelief, wonder, or all of them mixed together. Baba was recommended to the family by friends and even a clergyman secretly. Baba then grabbed his wrapper and tied it around his waist, unlike the first time when it was slung above one shoulder. His bare chest is covered with white, grotesque figures competing for the most awkward angles and postures. The old man doesn't look like a leopard slayer anymore. He whispers to the family:

'This thing no be our own. We neva see am before. Maybe oyinbo people go fit do am.' He then turns to his apprentice and orders him

'Give madam back her moni, no kolet anything from am again.'

Baba leads his acolyte out. The boy, about seven years of age, carries a calabash, a small talking drum, black leather bag and follows his mentor. Before leaving the hallway, Baba takes a long last look at Garba who looked one with the white padded room. The matriarch of the family starts weeping.

No one sees her come in until she is among the family. She puts a hand on Garba's mother and says "Mama, I came as soon as a friend told me. I know you don't know me but Garba has told me a lot about you."

'Who are you?' Mama asked.

'I am Emerald, Garba's special friend.'

END

RUFFLED BUTTERFLIES

'Will you marry me?'

'Em...em...ye...I don't...'

'Is that a Yes or a No?'

'Em...'

'My knee is beginning to hurt.'

'How much is that ring?'

'You'll find out when you accept it.'

'You know we still haven't ironed out some issues.'

'Issues? Like what?'

'I told you I want to go abroad for my master's.'

'Really? You can, after we get married.'

'My father said...'

'My father this, my daddy that. Must you bring your father into every discussion?'

'How can you say that? What do you have against my father and family?'

'Look here, if you want to marry your father, go ahead and leave me alone.'

'What? How can you even say that?'

'Yes, I will say it; you think I don't know of your father's plan to separate us?'

'That's not fair. My father is a good man.'

'Good man, I see.'

'On the contrary, it's your parents who don't like Okene girls.'

'I told you I'll handle my parents, just leave them to me.'

'The other day I took wrappers to your mother; she threw them back at me.'

'That was because you did not ask me. It was not a good time.'

'She is already against me; she will cause problems for us in future.'

'Wait a minute...I thought it was your master's you wanted us to iron out.'

'I have already been offered admission and will be leaving by the end of the year.'

'WHAT? You have already been what?'

'I wanted to tell you, but...'

'You wanted to tell me? But you didn't. I am sure you're going with your father.'

'Stop it, stop it! You knew when I was applying, why try and make it seem like I never mentioned it.'

'I am not listening to this.'

'Stop being childish; you know I love you.'

'Then let's get married.'

'How can I marry a man who doesn't want the best for me?'

'Says who? Of course, I want the best for you.'

'You don't share my dream of self-development and going abroad.'

'I have not said a thing like that!'

'You want me to sit at home and become your housewife.'

'I have not insinuated anything like that.'

'Then why are you kicking against my trip?'

'You want me to wait here for two years or more while you are abroad?'

'So, you mean you cannot be patient for me? How am I sure you are not already eyeing other girls?'

'You see? Suspicion. That has been the problem in this relationship.'

'But I didn't say I was suspecting you.'

'Then what did you say?'

'I am just asking why you are afraid to let me go abroad.'

'Can't you wait till next year? After we are married, then you can go?'

'Then you will be the one to sponsor my trip because my father will...'

'Oooh! This your father!'

'Leave my father alone.'

'I won't.'

'You will.'

'I can't.'

'You can, and you will. In fact, you must.'

'Tell your father I am bringing the customary kola and wine for your hand.'

'I will not tell him.'

'So now I know, you don't want to marry me.'

'I never said that.'

'Then tell him I am bringing wine, so he can drink and get drunk.'

'My father will not receive anything from a small boy.'

'What? Who are you calling a small boy?'

'I am not calling you a small boy.'

'Then what did you just say? 'Small boy!' Does your father have my type of car?'

'That's your business; my father is not as vain as you are.'

'See you; you don't like this car? Will you have looked my way if I didn't have a car?'

'I don't care. Our tradition permits me to only accept gifts from your parents.'

'You and your primitive tradition.'

'Yes, it's primitive, leave us alone.'

'You are not happy I want to marry such a bush girl like you.'

'That's the problem with you, you never address the issue.'

'If I have a problem, leave me alone and go abroad.'

'I have not said I want to leave you alone.'

'See, this thing is easy, let's get married at the registry then…'

'Fine! I like that idea.'

'So, have you accepted my ring?'

'No. We have not finished.'

'What other issues do you have in mind?'

'After the registry, I will not move into your house for…'

'What? What kind of marriage is that?'

'Listen first, before you start barking!'

'Barking. Oh, now I'm a dog.'

'No.'

'Then…'

'I think I need space. Maybe just leave me alone for a while.'

'Okay. Just I won't be here when you finish.'

'You see? I was right; you are already looking at small girls.'

'Yes, I am looking. After all, you called me a dog, what else do dogs do?'

'I am leaving.'

'Yes, go! You don't even do anything in the house.'

'If you had a problem with that why didn't you say something?'

'It's only fast food you know; I can't have kids eating only junk!'

'Don't I cook?'

'When? Where?'

'Can you say I have never cooked for you?'

'Please, you were on your way.'

'Yes, let me be going.'

'My parents warned me; I don't know why I didn't...'

'Yes, your parents are the ones interfering and not my father. But you keep saying it's my father.'

'Please go home, leave me alone.'

'I will not go anywhere until you tell me what your parents said.'

'This is not about my parents, see my ring.'

'Yes, I have seen it.'

'So?'

'So? Are you sure you will not take sides with your parents against me?'

'Are you sure your father will not marry you?'

'You are such a fool!'

'You are worse than a fool!'

[silence]

'Forget your father, and I will forget my parents.'

'I can't. I owe him a lot.'

'Okay, go abroad.'

'Do you really mean that?'

'Yes, you can go and study.'

'If you are asking me to go just because I said so, I won't, but if you mean it...'

'What do you want, again? I have said you can go.'

'No, you don't mean it.'

'Okay, I don't mean it.'

'Then why did you say you meant it?'

'You are just one crazy woman.'

'What do you think you are?'

'See you; you have put on the ring. After all your shakara.'

'Leave me alone.'

'So, you have accepted my proposal since you are wearing my ring?'

'Leave me alone.'

'Yeah.'

'Go away, I have not said yes.'

'Give me a hug...a kiss... something.'

'Get off me, you pervert!'

'So, will you marry me?'

'Do you really want to marry me?'

'It's up to you.'

'No, it's up to you.'

END

STAR BOY

Everyone who lived in the estate called Mike 'Star boy'. Mike became aware of the name one day as he drove out in the morning and some teenagers hailed him and waved. He didn't know he was that popular in the estate.

'You don't know? When your music disturbs the entire estate?' His wife asked him when he told her about the kids dancing 'shoki' and hailing him. It was part of the headache Sarah lived with every day. Women came to her complaining about her husband's loud music. Mike wouldn't have been bothering anyone if he didn't usually come home late at night. He would drive through the estate with very loud hip-hop music blasting from his speakers. Sarah pleaded with him to reduce the volume on his car stereo whenever he got close to the main entrance of the estate, but he didn't listen. His defence was that he never complained when neighbours left their generators on all night. He also never complained when there was a birthday party with little children dancing provocatively. Their parents never corrected them. Instead, they clapped and encouraged the little children to imitate flesh baring raunchy pop stars. Those people, Mike told Sarah, should not have a problem with him listening to music the way he liked.

Sarah knew Mike loved to party hard, but she had hoped he would stop after they got married. But four years had passed, and he was still rocking just as hard. She had tagged along for nights out in their first year but stopped when she became pregnant with their first child. The combination of cigarette smoke, perfume, sweat and alcohol was too much for her stomach. Mike initially went out to parties with Sarah's cousin saying she would keep an eye on him for his wife. They all laughed about Mike and his new club partner. When Sarah's cousin had to study for her exams, Mike went alone. It was his way of dealing with office pressure.

Mike was an aeronautical engineer with a multinational carrier and was well respected in the industry. He was the kind of person who never stopped when he set his mind on something. He was as sanguine as he was choleric, so he celebrated his successes. Despite being in his early forties, he could fit in a circle of university freshmen. Sarah was sometimes amused by how Mike still talked passionately about the things he talked about ten years ago when they started dating. He would tell her the RAM size, pixel quality and all the default apps of any cell phone he saw around. He would buy the phone only to give it out or sell it at a giveaway price and then go on to buy something more expensive. She set a mental timeline of six months for most of his gadgets. It was the same with his clothes, shoes and car. Well, his cars lasted two or three years. Sarah silently prayed that Mike wouldn't get tired of her and dispose of her like his gadgets. But her fears were beginning to materialise as she had caught him cheating a few times. It was heart-breaking. She couldn't understand why he did what he did, especially how he managed to balance devotion for her and their kids with a desire for bartenders. Mike had to have a fetish for barmaids, Sarah concluded. She couldn't figure out why he cheated on her with such women. He could afford to trip any high-class Milan model and spoil her with lavish gifts, but he stuck to ladies with no class. It had to be a fetish. He probably made them feel surreal around him, and they let down their guard; if they had any, to start with.

Sarah confirmed her troubles not long after their wedding when she accompanied Mike to watch a Champions League final. Sarah's defence went up the moment she noticed how a barmaid poured her husband's drink with a familiarity only women understand. The same barmaid poured her drink without looking her way. After the first drink, Mike excused himself, saying he had to use the restroom. At the corner of her eye, Sarah noticed the same barmaid serve some gentlemen before heading the same direction as her husband. The lounge was dimly lit with coloured lights which created a wonderful ambience. Sarah looked at her half empty glass and remembered some stories she heard about drug peddlers dropping pills in open glasses to get new addicts they would eventually supply. She quickly gulped the contents of her glass and headed to the restroom. There was a common foyer before the men and female convenience. And there was Mike, in a tight embrace with the barmaid. Sarah was transfixed as her husband's lips moved from the barmaid's ear to her neck. She walked back to her VIP corner and ordered another drink. Mike came back after a while explaining to his wife how he had had to use the toilet, blaming a sudden stomach upset on something he ate. He noticed how cold his wife was and tried to play her out of it. But Sarah was not impressed. Rather, she was irritated some more. When she couldn't take any more of his prancing, she poured the drink on his head and ordered him out of the lounge. Mike started complaining, but she walked out, and Mike followed her.

'What was that?' Mike asked.

'We've not been married for a year and you are already seeing other women?' Sarah shouted at Mike.

'I am not seeing someone else, how can you say that? Who feeds you with such malicious gossip?'

'What?' Sarah asked, incredulous. 'Take me home please. Now!'

Mike acceded; Sarah cried all the way home.

Sarah lived the following week like she was the only one in the house. She stopped cooking for Mike and doing his laundry. It was the fact that Mike could look her in the eyes and lie that stung her more than his infidelity. He was the one who made a vow to God to forsake all other women and cling to his wife; if he decided to break that vow, it was between him and his maker. But to lie and play on her intelligence, that was another issue. The cataclysmic effect a lie had was that it shattered the outer walls of a person, leaving them exposed. For Sarah, the man in her husband was gone; his education and elitist stature counted for nothing. He had reduced himself to a liar, petty criminal, drug peddler, riff-raff, rogue, lout, agbero… and all such things. She wondered how she could be yoked to such a person for the rest of her life. After all the painstaking pruning of her male friends, she still ended up with a cheating, lying man for a husband.

Sarah knew she couldn't keep living like she was and decided to make her home a happy place. She walked up to Mike who was playing a video game in the living room. She grabbed the remote control and turned off the TV and spoke:

'Look here Mr Man, if you think I got married to you to have a miserable time, you are wrong. I do not accept your creeping around with that bartender and making a fool of me. What do you see in that girl that you flirt with her in public? You must change, or I will leave you.' As she said this, she swung her right hand and slapped Mike, twaark! She gave him another slap with her left hand! Mike noticed that the energy in her left hand was not as strong as her right hand, so the slap was not as powerful. Sarah did not know where this slapping came from as it was not part of her plans. As she stood looking down at him, some emotion took over her and she started to cry. 'See what you have made me do,' she said.

Mike didn't know what to make of his wife's slaps. He knew he was guilty, so he just held on to the game pad knowing he deserved what came to him. From his sitting position, he saw his wife like a grizzly bear with huge paws and sharp claws. Twaark! One more slap from the grizzly bear with an accompanying roar. He could see the bear now in slow motion, the gradual raise of both hands in the air and a slow blow to his face. He must have received six slaps before he protested. Sarah started to cry and told him to see what he made her do. Mike thought he would just face the issue.

'Why can't you accept me the way I am?' Mike asked his wife.

'What?' Sarah was stunned. 'Mike, are you listening to yourself?'

'Some people are born with sickle cell anaemia, others are born with rickets. Should they kill themselves because they are that way? I was born with a soft spot for women and ...'

Twaaark!!! Sarah handed Mike another slap to correct his thoughts. She walked away from him knowing that her problems were greater. For her husband to see his actions as natural, it meant she had a lot of work ahead of her.

Sarah had heard her friends say that men were all the same, and that the sooner a woman realised, the better for blood pressure. She did not, however, believe in that generalisation. She knew it was a mindset and could be conditioned or changed. She consoled herself that since her husband had made such a confession, it was a step in the right direction and resolved to make him recondition his mind.

Sarah was confused. She didn't know what approach would work best for her husband. If she marked him too closely, he could feel suffocated and recede from her. She had read books about relationships and all she had gathered was that no two marriages are the same. She also learnt that different things worked for different couples. She had to find out what would make her marriage work. First, she needed Mike to tell her why he married her. From childhood, Sarah had dreamed of a happy marriage. She remembered watching cartoons where lovely princesses met their prince charming. Sarah decided that she had to have her prince charming. Even if Mike was a frog or a toad, she would kiss him till he transformed into a tall, handsome prince.

The following day, she drove her car to her mechanic and told him she wanted to leave the car with him for a couple of days. He could use it to run his errands; she didn't mind. Later that day, she called Mike and told him that her car had developed a fault and that she would need a ride home from her office. From that day, Mike drove her to work and picked her up in the evenings for a week. It was as if having separate cars had kept them apart and they didn't bond as much. She started packing him a lunch box to take to work and an extra pack for his secretary, Alice. She also checked up on Alice occasionally. She got Alice a present on her birthday and helped with some extra cash for her groceries. Sarah noticed how reluctant Alice was to collect anything from her, but she shrugged it off as part of the girl's humility.

Sarah got a call from Alice one day and hoped that nothing was wrong. Alice insisted she had something to tell Sarah in person, so they fixed a lunch date. Both ladies met at a restaurant, and Alice picked a table around the playpen section of the restaurant; she knew it was a school day, so they would not be disturbed. Sarah exuded her usual lovely cheer, but Alice was downcast and would not look up.

'Alice, I hope everything is alright.' Sarah started the conversation.

'I am fine ma,' Alice said. She took out some tissue paper from her purse and started crying, blowing her nose noisily. Sarah shifted her chair closer to the girl and put a hand on her shoulder. Sarah figured that whatever the girl had to say, she would say in her own time since she was the one who called for the meeting.

Alice gathered herself and spoke. 'Ma, my name is Ifeoma, not Alice. My former boss at the bar called me Alice. He said it had a soft feel and would make customers like me. Ma, I sold drinks at a number of bars until I met your husband. Since the first day you sent a lunch pack to me in the office, I have felt guilty and uncomfortable. I always thought you were mean and overbearing, but I see I have just been fooling myself. Ma, I am so sorry I have been hurting you. I met your husband one day at the bar. I was supposed to make a customer feel good by allowing him to slap my buttocks, but I refused, and my boss started to hit me. Your husband ran to my rescue by attacking my boss. He beat the stupid man up and pushed him into a garbage can. He then picked me up and took me to a hospital. He checked up on me while I was there and took care of all medical bills. Before I was discharged from the hospital, your husband asked me where he could drop me off, and I told him that I had slept in all the bars where I worked. I didn't have any relatives in Lagos. He then took me to one of his colleagues' house. He said I wouldn't stay there for a long time. And as he promised, he got me an apartment. It was a single room with a toilet and a kitchen. Madam, your husband came to see me at home a number of times, and I started cooking for him, enjoying his company. After some weeks, he offered me a job. Since then, I have felt indebted to him and thought that if he wanted to be with me, it must be because he didn't have a good wife. I now know that I am very wrong ma, and I'm sorry for being with your husband.'

Sarah was quiet throughout the narration by Alice or Ifeoma. Her first thought was 'That's my Prince Charming.' She knew that was Mike alright, to go out of his way to be chivalrous. She felt proud of her husband and wondered if that was the appropriate feeling to have after listening to a young woman who just said she had been having an affair with her husband. Sarah hugged Ifeoma, and both ladies cried in each other's embrace.

Alice resigned the next day, leaving Mike in shock. She didn't say why she was leaving or where she was leaving for. She simply packed her things out of her apartment and disappeared, giving only Sarah her new phone number and getting her to promise not to give it to Mike.

Sarah lived a happier life after Alice disappeared and her husband seemed to behave himself. Mike became a changed man and spent more time with Sarah. Sarah decided to make her marriage work despite her husband's escapades. They shared meals at restaurants, snacked on a lot of sugary food and went out a lot more. Life was like the cartoons Sarah watched.

Unknown to Sarah, Mike was going through a hard time. Six peaceful months had passed before Sarah got a call from a police station one Saturday night. She learnt from the police officer that her husband had been rounded up with some people at an illegal brothel and had to be bailed before that night. If he was not bailed that night, he would have to sleep in a holding cell till Monday and may be charged to court. Mike had called to say he would work late, and she had said okay. She had not known that he had other designs. That night, she drove quietly to the police station and told the officer on duty why she was there. As a female police officer brought out a form for Sarah to fill, she became talkative.

'Madam, what is your relationship with this man?'

'He is my husband, officer,' Sarah replied.

'I have seen many things with my eyes as an officer, and I know I don't like where I saw your husband. Something inside me said I should call you, if not, we for detain am till Monday, come charge am go court.'

'Thank you, officer, God bless you,' Sarah said and reached into her purse to give the officer some money.

'Madam, e nor necessary. Hold your moni. I be woman like you and me sef want beta tin for my house. You know as this men dem be. Carry your husband go house make you take care of am. Nothing wey e dey find for that place wey you nor get.' Sarah was touched by the officer and wondered why people had negative things to say about the police; she had just witnessed love and kindness despite the general disregard meted to the police.

'Madam, your husband say na party dem dey do for where we catch them. That place no be party place. In short, we get intelligence for that place. And the report no good. As we check your husband ID card, we see say na better person. Make you de draw him ear for house. My sister, you hear me so?'

Sarah stared at the form in front of her and kept answering, 'Yes officer,' as the officer spoke.

Mike was brought out of his holding cell a little groggy. He was trying very hard to put on his shirt and slip his belt through the belt holes of his trousers at the same time. Sarah watched him with utter disgust. Mike didn't attempt to put on his socks. Perhaps, he knew he could not retain his balance, so he stuffed the socks into his trouser pocket. Sarah could hear shrills of ladies in the cell where

Mike came out from. They were pleading to be bailed as well. One lady was waving her multi-coloured wig frantically through the bars to be noticed. As Mike got closer to Sarah, she smelled urine, alcohol, and filth on him. His eyes were red and glazed as he tried very hard to keep them open.

As Sarah drove home, she kept wondering if her husband had started abusing drugs. That would be a difficult turn of events in their lives.

'Mr Man,' she started. She always called him that when there was trouble, or when she rebuffed his actions. 'Mr Man, have you started taking drugs?' she asked.

Mike did not answer, so she thought better of asking him questions in his current state. She knew he was out celebrating his departure from the country. Mike was one of the privileged few to get a three-month grant at a research institute in Malaysia. She was happy for him, but she feared what he would do with himself there.

Initially, when Sarah got the call from the police station, she had been terrified. She had heard stories of people abducted days before they travelled out of the country. They had a neighbour who had packed his bags, ready to travel, only for him to be attacked and carted away a day before his departure. The robbers dropped the man in some remote location and made away with his car, phone and bags. Everyone suspected the security guard to be the mole; he was later taken away by the police for questioning.

Sarah had constantly cautioned Mike about running his mouth. She thought it wise to tell no one, except close family members that he was travelling abroad. But Mike thought differently. He almost made it a point of reference whenever he talked to his friends. Sarah could not believe it one day, when Mike revealed his plans to a roadside vulcanizer. The car's back tyre had picked up a nail and the air was running out fast, so they decided to get it fixed. As the vulcaniser beat out the tyre from the rim, they watched him place a patch and heat it up with fire; he then took out a ball of *Eba* from a polythene bag and smeared it all round the tyre to act as a sealant. That was when Mike spoke:

'Ah! This can only happen in Nigeria. Who tell you say *Eba* dey gum tyre? When I enter Malaysia next week, I go find better technology come show una, no be dis yeye-yeye thing wey una dey do.'

Sarah knew her husband wasn't going to bring anything new to change the face of vulcanising in Nigeria. He was boasting, and she was worried. If Mike could massage his ego that way in front of someone he hardly knew, she wondered how he behaved after a few drinks at the bar.

Sarah was very relieved, though unhappy, when she discovered that she was only called to bail Mike. She saw binge drinking as something teenagers did to try to fit in, but for someone of her husband's stature, it didn't make sense. She had tried a little drinking while she was in the university but didn't like the taste. For beer to become an acquired taste, one had to tolerate its bitter taste for a while. She thought of guys during her secondary school days who made sure they broke school rules to feel cool. At that time, it seemed the more rules one broke, the cooler one became. A group of boys would not tuck in their shirts on the assembly ground. After they had been picked out and told to dress properly, the boys would only tuck in the front of their shirt to reveal an amazingly large belt buckle and leave the backs of their shirts flying. Such boys often wore black socks instead of white saying white was childish, as were sandals. They would rather wear leather flip flops without socks. After such behaviour attracted suspension from the school authority, the offenders became heroes, and getting suspended became the ticket to join their exclusive club. Sarah looked at her husband like a rebellious school boy. But the important question she wanted him to answer was: what or who was he rebelling against?

Mike travelled for his studies the following week, and Sarah felt very light, like a huge weight had rolled off her shoulders. She had gone through a lot on his behalf and began to see things from her friend's perspective, that she should threaten a divorce even if she didn't want to go through it. Sarah contemplated this move, knowing that Mike could just say 'fine, that's all I've been looking for,' and her bluff would rebound. Now, he was going off for three months, Sarah hoped that their marriage would not be the worse for it...

Three months passed and Mike returned to Nigeria a different man. He was less talkative and had picked up some polite manners. Sarah woke up to the smell of very strong and strange spices the morning after her husband's arrival. She heard pots and pans clanking with an occasional roar of sizzling oil. She fought hard not to jump out of bed to investigate what Mike was up to, so as not to ruin his surprise. Mike came into the room with food on a tray and proudly presented the *Roti Canai* to his wife. Sarah pretended to have just woken up from sleep as he placed the tray beside her. She pulled on the astonishingly stretchy pancake look-alike. There was also a small soup bowl decorated with Asian motifs holding the strongest curry she had perceived, and its taste was heavenly. As they ate, Mike told her how he enjoyed this as breakfast in Malaysia and told her of its Indian ancestry. Sarah also got to like the taste of *Asam Jala* and *Nasi Lemak*. She made sure she wore one of the dresses he got her to work on Fridays. Her colleagues loved the feel of the fabric, and Sarah loved how airy the clothes were, though they still covered her nicely.

Mike was her darling once more. He took her out to watch movies at a cinema at least once in a month. He wrote poems and tucked them in her shoes or jacket pockets. Sarah was often delighted to stumble on something Mike had written. He was even more wonderful with the kids. He got complicated remote-controlled toy planes and trucks for the boy and life-sized dolls for the girl. It was like he used the kids as an excuse to buy toys for himself. He and the kids spent hours rolling on the floor, mimicking machines and acting out a series of their own imagined versions of stories. Mike's work had some dry spells, and he found a new way of utilising this time. He stayed at home more than before his trip and it was beautiful for Sarah. She loved to call the house phone during the day to speak to her kids and then hear his voice in the background. Sarah lived her fairytale life for a little over four months before the shocker of her life.

'I don die! I don die! Hei, I don die ooo!' Mike covered his head with a blanket trying not to watch the scenes panning over and over on the TV. He suddenly felt sick and curled on the bed foetus like. The young lady he was with in the hotel room came out of the bathroom and asked what he was shouting about. Mike didn't uncover himself; he just kept muttering, 'I done die' over and over. The young lady could not make out what he was saying but looked at the TV set and saw the news of a plane crash.

Earlier that day, Sarah had driven Mike to the airport; he was to catch a flight to a business meeting in Abuja. She had waited with him until they heard the boarding announcement for his flight. She watched him check in and get his boarding pass, and since the departure lounge was strictly for travellers, she couldn't proceed. They hugged and she left the airport. Mike watched as his wife left the lounge before heading out of the airport. He had told Sarah he was spending two days in Abuja and needed to travel light. He slung his bag across his shoulder, popped the collar of his polo T-shirt, put on his Ray bans, and swaggered out of the airport. He hailed a cab and asked to be taken to a hotel close by.

Back home, Sarah stared as the TV reporter talked about probable causes of the plane's inability to fully take off resulting in the crash. She could not make sense of 'speculations to a disintegrating fan blade… black box recovery will prove most pertinent for any investigations…calculations as to the total weight of the plane and the length of the runway… clear skies for the better part of the morning…'

'We'd like to, but cannot rule out pilot incompetence until we are sure of the cause of this crash. We will be examining the flight manifest to ascertain the number of passengers on board and get in touch with their families.' The white expats on the TV looked like janitors wearing overalls with unkempt bushy hair and thick rimmed glasses, not Harvard graduates. She could not come to terms with the fact that she was watching the wreck of the plane her husband was on. It had been barely two hours since she left him, which means the plane went down around when she stopped to buy bread at the neighbourhood store. Sarah was devastated and crumbled to the floor.

In Mike's hotel room, a different drama was playing out. While Mike was shouting that he had died, he farted. The thing was loud and long and smelled terribly. He gripped his stomach, but his half-worn trousers hindered his movement, and he could not make it to the toilet early enough. So, he shat himself in his pants, right in the middle of the room. Perhaps it was the stench of his corruption forcefully exiting his system or the realisation that he could have died if he really had been on that flight that made him whimper.

The last time Mike cried was years ago, when he was a broke student and had tried to sleep in a bar. The barmaids had driven him out, locked their shop and told him that the fact that he bought some miserable beer did not entitle him to turn the bar into his home. They had shaken their behinds at him and left him in the cold. That night, he had made a silent vow that he would be rich; to conquer as many barmaids as possible.

The smell of Mike's waste quickly filled the room and became too much for his guest to handle. She did not even know his name. All she had got from her friend who hooked her up was 'Meet my friend; take care of him well o, he is a very big boy.' Here she was, with the big boy who behaved like an infant. She wanted nothing to do with cleaning his slew, or even answering any questions, so she slipped into her clothes, picked Mike's wallet from his trousers and removed all the cash. She then wished him all the best and left.

The news of the plane crash spread like wildfire and those who knew people on the flight or frequent fliers started calling their loved ones. Sarah's sister did not bother calling, she sped to the house and found her sister crumbled on the floor holding what looked like a barmaid dress. Sarah had ordered a barmaid dress for herself. It would be Mike's birthday soon, and she planned to give him a special treat. Sarah and her sister started wailing miserably, and their neighbours soon started checking in to find out the cause of the noise.

Sarah's phone was ringing but she didn't want to pick up. It was probably someone who had heard the news and wanted to confirm and sympathise. But she stopped. The ringtone was Chidinma's *I've Fallen in Love with You*, and it was the special ringtone she used for her husband only. She picked the call and threatened the person at the other end.

'Hello. Hello. This is my husband's phone. You are a thief; you must have stolen it at the airport. Scoundrel, if you know what is good for you, return my husband's phone, you…' Sarah broke down in tears.

The neighbours watched, incredulous; until Frank, the neighbour from the flat upstairs took the phone. He spoke in a harsh manly voice.

'Hello who are you and how did you get this phone?' Frank listened for what seemed like an eternity, and then dropped the call. 'I'll be back,' he said, 'pull yourself together.' Frank signalled to another man and they stepped outside together.

Mike knew it wasn't right to allow his wife grieve over his death when he was yet alive. So he called thinking that Sarah would be happy. But Sarah had threatened him, calling him a thief and an impostor and asked him to return the phone. He could barely make sense of what Sarah had said, and all efforts to get her to listen failed. The woman was hysterical and might have started cursing him before a man took the phone and listened calmly. His phone rang again, and Mike gave his neighbour, Mr Frank, the address of the hotel he was in at Ikeja. Mike bundled his soiled clothes into a corner and changed into fresh clothes. He had cleaned up as much as he could. He would leave and let room service deal with the rest. By the time they found out, he'd be long gone.

Soon, Frank and another man knocked on the door, and Mike asked them in. The first thing they perceived was the smell.

'Starboy,' Frank called with a scrunched up nose, 'you are alive. How did you do it? Your wife said you were on that flight.'

'Long story my brother, long story. I was really supposed to be on that flight, but I took a wrong turn,' Mike said.

'Wrong turn?' Frank said. 'And what's stinking in here?' Frank and his friend looked around.

'Mr Frank,' Mike said, 'thank you for coming through. About the smell, it's a long story. I'm sure room service can deal with it after I leave. About the wrong turn, that was my making.' Mike proceeded to tell Frank and the other man about how he felt stifled because his wife kept dogging his footsteps. He told the men how he had actually bought a flight ticket but had not even intended to travel. It was true that his wife watched him go into the departure lounge, but he had left the airport after he watched his wife take her leave. He had made a quick detour to rendezvous with a girl he had met at a bar. Then the news of the plane crash broke.

Frank was disgusted. So, in addition to playing loud music on the street at night, Mike also womanised. 'You certainly have some explaining to do to your wife,' he said.

Mike nodded. 'Yes. Yes, I do and I will. For God's sake, I could have been on that flight and perished like the others for no reason.'

'We should go,' Frank said. 'Let's get you home?' Before they left, Frank sent a message to his own wife asking her to comfort Sarah, that her husband was alive.

When they arrived, Sarah sat, quiet, looking at her husband. Then, suddenly, she ran to him and held him. 'I thought I had lost you,' she cried. Frank coughed. Sarah spoke again. I heard them call your flight; I saw you go in. What happened?

'Last minute change of plans,' Mike answered.

'Last minute change of plans?' Sarah said, 'And you couldn't call me?'

'Shhhh, I'm here now.'

'Hmmn,' Frank cleared his voice. 'Congratulations Mr and Mrs Starboy. God will always keep us safe. We'll be leaving now.'

'Thank you,' Mike said to the neighbours as they left.

'Starboy,' another neighbour called, 'can you please turn down your music when you drive in at night?'

Mike nodded. He would turn down the music; he didn't want his neighbours wishing he had really died.

As soon as the neighbours left, Mike decided to come clean; he sat down to tell his wife what really happened.

END

MR. AND MRS. MORGAN

April 27th was gloriously sunny in the morning. The grass had turned lush green after receiving just four rains in the year. The air was pure as if it had been freshly released from a large purification tank somewhere in the clouds. To a first timer from Lagos or any other part of the country, the fresh air on the plateau felt like condensed elixir to first cleanse their lungs before re-liquefying to elongate their lives. The hills rolled as far as the eyes could see and simply summarised the beauty of nature untouched. This was the attraction for the Morgans before they built their retirement home in Vom, on the outskirts of Jos. The architect who handled the construction of the house surpassed Mr Morgan's dreams of a cottage. The stone work that formed the foundation of the building was well laid by great stone masons and well elevated above ground level. The French windows allowed the sun to come into their living room and sit with them till late in the evening. The house had a fireplace where they could build a fire against the harmattan cold as each year drew close. The cottage was fitted with inverters and solar panels to meet their power needs and a borehole out back to provide portable water. There was a functional mix of different architectural eras with the cottage. The interior had lovely Plaster of Paris ceilings and cornices on the wall. The tiling of the kitchen was exquisite with a touch of modern cooker hood. There was a pond not far from the house where the Morgans installed a submersible pump that irrigated their garden all year round.

Mr and Mrs Morgan loved to sit out in the gazebo to bask in the picturesque surroundings. Whenever the sun rose, beauty rose radiating the green grass, brown metal railings, lettuce, spinach, and sunflower all embracing the sun. Every morning, Mr Morgan released his rabbits from their hutch and watched them skip to nibble the freshly cut cabbage and lettuce he had spread out for them. Mrs Morgan would be in the garden as was usual at that time of the morning. She grew almost everything she wanted: green peas, pepper, carrots, radishes, cabbage, lettuce, and okra. The garden was amazing, so they rarely drove to the markets in town for groceries.

The Morgans were both well over sixty and retired, so they spent a lot of time together at home adoring each other and reliving their youth. Mr Morgan had been an accountant with a private auditing firm and put in close to thirty years before retiring. Mrs Morgan, on the other hand, had been a lecturer at the University of Jos and retired as a Reader. They had two children, both married; one lived in Monaco while the other lived in Lisbon. Occasionally, the Morgans travelled to see their children and grandchildren. When they were not travelling, their children insisted on sending money and pictures back home. Pictures, Mr and Mrs Morgan wanted; money, they didn't need. They were comfortable and content.

The Morgans had been thinking about adopting a child or two, and the morning of April 27th felt like a good time to make a move. Both Mr and Mrs Morgan believed that they were in a privileged position to help those in need. But there was also another reason to consider adoption: they missed running after kids in panic knowing that a child could clip his fingers in the door hinge. They missed being responsible and alert to the needs of children. What like the trouble of children to enliven a beautiful house and elongate one's life?

Mr and Mrs Morgan had heard that there was an orphanage close by. Talk about the orphanage often featured in their friends' discourse, so the Morgans decided to visit. They would acquaint themselves with the process of adoption and be advised about the right age of children that an aging couple could keep.

The drive to the orphanage was rather exciting and full of expectation. When they arrived, the kids were having a late breakfast. Breakfast was particularly late that day because there had been prolonged prayers that morning for the new kids who would be joining the orphanage later in the day. There were the little children who had to be looked after, and there were older children who could look after themselves and other children. The children did not have the best clothes, but they were not in rags. One got the feeling that the orphanage did its best with its meagre resources and the goodwill they received from well-intentioned people.

The Morgans were taken round the facility by the founder of the orphanage, Ms Ada, and were very impressed with what they saw. They wondered what they had been doing not to have visited earlier. They presented their gifts and requested a private meeting with Ms Ada; she acquiesced.

'How do you manage to feed all the children you have here?' Mrs Morgan asked as soon as they sat down.

Ada blushed a little before responding. 'God is always faithful. Somehow, He provides, and we never run out of food.' She opened her palms to the sky. 'We are also grateful to good people like you who donate generously.'

Mr Morgan wanted to know if the children went to school and how Ada coped.

'Well,' Ada answered, 'all our children go to school. The truth is this: a small donation of one thousand naira goes a long way in the lives of these kids.' Ada quietly went into a careful breakdown of how much she spent on each kid per term in school. Mr and Mrs Morgan listened, awed. The work Ada and her team did was simply magical.

'Sorry if I'm asking too many questions…'

'It's not a bother, Mrs Morgan,' Ada answered.

Mrs Morgan smiled. 'So, how do you get these kids?'

Ada had anticipated this question; it was one that she was asked often.

'We go around a lot of IDP camps in the state. We pick up children with no one to look after them. Most of these children you see here have lost both parents. Some of them suffer untold hardship in the camps at the hands of people with whom they share a bond of suffering. And, usually, they have no one to defend them, neither can they look after themselves. There is only so much we can do, but we do our bit.

Mr and Mrs Morgan kept quiet. They were still under the spell of this woman who knew the limits of her intervention but still would not be deterred. What difference did thirty-two children make out of all the thousands, possibly millions, of children orphaned in the state? What difference would adopting a child, or two, or maybe ten children make? These thoughts ran through the Morgans' mind in fractions.

Ms Ada, wondering about the silence of this couple thought

they were waiting to hear more. So, she told them about what went on in the lives of the children and in the IDP camps.

'Sometimes, these children, especially the girls, think they are responsible for the death of their parents and become introverts during their teenage years. Some of them were molested by their relatives and elders while they were at the IDP camps. Without a parent or guardian, some children in the camps sleep in the open, exposed to the elements. Some of them have to barter their bodies to get food. If they don't, they get raped anyway. I have two kids here, a boy and a girl, children of the same parents, who did unimaginable things. They saw their incestuous behaviour as normal when they were just twelve and nine years old, because it was everywhere around them.

'We have lectures for the adults in such devastated areas. We sensitise and even encourage the men to marry even more than one wife, but they should leave the children alone. It is just sickening how some men take advantage of these little children. From the security men, to highly placed men in the society. I'm sorry sir, but some men are animals. Before we bring any child here, we run a series of medical tests and most times we record cases of STDs. These children are also abused by women too. You know, those women who sometimes come from Lagos in search of girls they can use as housemaids. I'm sure you've been listening to the news sir, and you know how bad life can be for those housemaids. So, sir, to every child that is saved, it makes a difference to that child.'

Mr and Mrs Morgan were shocked beyond words. They were not even sure if it was right to ask another question. They were also unsure of whom to offer comfort, the children or Ms Ada. Help is good, it always comes from a good place, but it can be abstract and characterless. But comfort has all the ingredients – coming from a good place and not lacking in character and personal touch. Ada's phone rang, and she excused herself to take the call. When she returned, she asked the Morgans if they wanted to come along with her to go and pick up some children from a village not far away. The Morgans agreed. Such was their awe of the woman.

Ada swung her car towards the Yakubu Gowon Airport to first pick up some of her benefactors who were flying in from Abuja. They then set off from Heipang through Bisichi to the IDP camp in Dyenbruk, somewhere in Jos South. They journeyed through breath-taking landscape that could have been explored as a source of eco-tourism. One amazing thing Mrs Morgan noticed was that women sat on rocks breaking them into smaller gravel bits that trucks came to buy for construction sites. It was mind-boggling how those women sat all day breaking stones and then sold them for peanuts. Women also heaped sacks and sacks of Irish potatoes by the road for sale alongside an unending display of fresh shiny fruit and vegetables in baskets. Ada stopped by the road and asked for Mama Godiya who sold two big bags of potatoes at an amazingly low price. The visitors from Abuja ordered two more bags for themselves, knowing the fortune it would have cost back home.

There had been a massacre of hundreds of women and children in Dogo na Hauwa a week before, and Ada wanted to get first hand understanding of the place to know the type of intervention to bring and which affiliate organisation to bring on board. Stories about such places were often exaggerated or misrepresented by social media, hence the importance of personal visits. From a distance, they could all see smoke from what was left of some thatch houses and wondered what could make a fire stay on for so long after the attacks. Perhaps, a fire set with evil intent took more time to go out. People were gathered in clusters, and the atmosphere was heavy with sorrow and grief. For those who still wailed, their voices were faint. Apart from the faint wailing, the place was silent.

As Ada's entourage got closer, they had to stop in front of large boulders the villagers had used as checkpoint barricades. Ada got out and hung a tag around her neck indicating she was part of a humanitarian aid group the community had come to recognise. She spoke Berom, though she was Igbo, greeting and consoling the villagers.

About seven men formed a semicircle, and as Mr Morgan walked closer to them, he could see what lay in front of them. There were three headless bodies on the ground. The bodies were so small they should have belonged to toddlers. Mrs Morgan started crying and vomiting. Her husband was lucky he had only a glass of juice that morning, or he would have also lost it like she just did. Mrs Morgan retched, and her stomach hurt as there was nothing left there to throw up. She could taste bile in her mouth and asked to be taken back to the car. Before Mr Morgan could grab his wife by the hand, she had crumbled to the fine dusty sand and cried. Catarrh rolled freely from her nose. Mrs Morgan's troubles increased as she tried to stand up and caught sight of an arm that had been cut off from somewhere above the elbow next to her. She screamed and rolled away. It was a wave of grief, sorrow, heartache, anguish, pain, misery, woe, all in one.

A dry elderly man wearing a dirty and torn dashiki welcomed Ada and her friends. He was shrivelled and had no more than ten red teeth left in his mouth which he constantly used to chew kolanuts. He had lost two wives, four children and seven grandchildren in attacks on their community so far. He was the village head. Mr Morgan thought to himself that they should have been the ones consoling these villagers, but the villagers were the ones consoling and welcoming visitors. The village head was speaking, '...we are sad, but God gives, and he takes.' Mr Morgan was amazed that the villagers did not nurse any bestial feelings against their attackers. All the houses were gutted. It was as if bulldozers had run over the village leaving destruction and death in their wake. Mud houses were reduced to rubble. Broken pots and plates littered the place. One could see branches and leaves used to cover corpses. Bodies were wrapped in cloth with stones used as pegs to hold down the edges of the wrappers. The usual 'unknown gunmen' had run through the village in their numbers without a trace. There was something odd Mr Morgan noticed; there were no animals around. A typical village like this should have had chickens, goats, dogs, ducks and pigs roaming around but there was none in sight through the period of their visit. Could the animals have foreseen this dread and fled?

Mr Morgan excused himself from Ada's company and went to join his wife inside the car; he had to get the weight off his legs and feet. Mrs Morgan still felt sore and a fresh rawness in her throat. After a while, Ada came back and said they had to head back into town. The ride back was not as exciting as the ride to the ravaged village. No one admired the scenery of the hills or bought any more produce at a cheap price.

Ada offered an adoption form to the Morgans when they got back to the orphanage. Mrs Morgan had stretched her hand to receive the form when her husband held her hand back and said they would give it some more thought. He promised they would pay the orphanage another visit soon. They said their goodbyes and the Morgans drove to their cottage, very sorrowful.

The weather had changed as they were approaching their house, heavy black clouds had gathered, and it looked like it would rain heavily. The rains started as the Morgans got into the house. It was easy for the Morgans to predict what was on each other's mind as they ate quietly that night. They intuitively did not talk about the adoption plan that day; instead, they spent time on the phone with their children and grandkids, talking about everything except their visit to the orphanage.

The next morning, as the Morgans sat down to breakfast; Mrs Morgan asked her husband why he thought a nice young woman like Ada was unmarried. Mr Morgan shrugged and said nothing. Mrs Morgan noticed that her husband wasn't particularly chatty that morning but still probed.

'Honey, why did you stop me from collecting the adoption form from Ada yesterday?'

'I don't know. Something just didn't feel right. I didn't feel like it was the right thing to do anymore after everything we saw yesterday.'

Mrs Morgan was not pleased with his answer. There had to be more, and she wanted to know.

'But from what we saw, I was more determined to change the life of at least one child before I go to heaven,' Mrs Morgan said.

'How do you correct or mould the mind of such a child?' Mr Morgan asked.

'I don't understand what you mean,' his wife enquired.

'Erm, how do I put it without sounding dramatic? Those children are gone; mentally, I mean. It's not that I am giving up on them, but I don't see how I can bring up such children in my house. I don't even have the youth required to bring them up. Let's leave them to the professionals; we will keep donating what we can.'

Mrs Morgan didn't agree with her husband's views, but she knew better than arguing. She didn't quite understand why he felt differently. They had wanted to adopt a child to give a better chance at life. Also, she had nursed the thoughts of raising a child from its infancy. She also had thoughts of going to work for Ada, perhaps on the weekends, without pay, like the volunteers she had met on their last visit.

Mrs Morgan didn't bring up the adoption topic for a week and thought of a different approach to the whole thing. Even after a week, she couldn't still understand her husband's decision, since he was the first to talk about adoption before she caught the bug and wanted to run with it. Her plan was simple; she wanted him to see things from a different perspective. The opportunity came one day when their inverter batteries didn't have enough power to light up the whole house. Mr and Mrs Morgan sat outside the house, each thinking different thoughts.

Mrs Morgan wanted to tell her husband a story about something in her childhood that she wasn't quite sure about. She remembered, or thought she remembered, an instance when she was abused as a child. She once woke up, or thought she woke up, and found her elder brother touching her pudenda. She was nine years or so at the time. But she had been sleepy and not sure. When she woke up the next day to confront her brother, he denied and asked her if she was sure it was not a dream. And what devilish thoughts must she have to make her dream such terrible things? She wasn't sure, so she was ashamed and had kept quiet. One weekend, they had relatives stay over in their house. She had this uncle who kept calling her 'my wife.' He put her in his lap that evening and kept shifting her against his groin. She had been uncomfortable and tried to move away, but the uncle had held her in a firm grip. She eventually freed herself but had told no one.

'Honey,' Mrs Morgan began, I don't think I can remember vividly, but I think I was abused as a child.' Mr. Morgan looked up sharply and asked his wife what exactly she meant. 'I have never told anyone, but when I was younger, we had some relatives who stayed at our house, and for some reason, one of my uncles kept calling me 'my wife'. I didn't know the relationship between us, but I know he kept calling me his wife. One weekend he put me on his thighs…'

Mr Morgan held up his hand. 'I know our visit to the orphanage affected you strongly. That's why you are telling me these stories now. Please, this thing you are about to say has been a secret for long, let it remain so. We'll do what we can for those children.'

END

ELECTRONIC LISTS

Jide parked his 2002 Honda Accord, popularly called *baby boy*, beside the road in front of the last provision store before turning to his street. He checked his phone to verify if his wife had sent him a WhatsApp message, a text or an email. It was drizzling, but he could quickly dash into the store to buy whatever his wife wanted. He checked his phone carefully and was satisfied that she hadn't sent a list. However, he got out of his car to buy a recharge card for his phone: he didn't like going to bed knowing he wouldn't be able to communicate with anyone in the case of a night emergency. Before going back to his car, he decided to grab a quick smoke, so he bought a stick and cut it into half, throwing the top half away. That was his way of cutting down and hopefully quitting. He took three long drags and handed the butt to a bystander who was looking longingly at the cigarette.

Jide turned off the main road onto the bumpy dirt road that led to his house. He had the same thoughts every night as he drove home: to move into a different part of town where the roads were tarred all the way to his gate. Because of the rain, he had to be more careful dodging potholes. The potholes were indiscernible, and a miscalculation could see him losing his exhaust pipe in the mud. He felt the bottom plate of the car grate against the bumpy road and it felt like it was his belly rubbing against the hard road. He hated it. He had run into trouble once on that stretch of road when, just before he got to his house, the bottom of his fuel tank hit a stone and ruptured. That was the day he knew the danger of caked mud underneath a car.

Apart from the bad road, Jide did not like the garbage heaps scavenged by dogs, chickens, rodents and other vermin. He had once called a garbage disposal company to clear the heaps, and they erected signposts saying, 'no refuse here by order,' after clearing the entire street. Two days later, the street was back to its usual dirty self — the signposts that read 'no refuse here by order,' were dressed in polythene bags of different colours like scarecrows. He had taken care of the bill hoping that when people in the community saw what had happened, they would be more cautious as to how they handled their trash. He had wanted it to be the start of a community self-help initiative. He also wanted it to kick-start awareness on street cleanliness. He had planned to notify each house along the street about how much it would cost them to contribute to have a truck regularly come to remove their trash. Unfortunately, nobody asked how the truck came about cleaning. He spoke to the youth leader and asked him to bring it up in their meetings. They youths responded that they did not have money for such a venture. The one time anyone made a comment about his gesture, it was to ask: 'Who is this guy, and which political office is he seeking? Is he a son of the soil? Which party is he?' Jide had been sad and embarrassed.

Embarrassment and shame converged on Jide when a colleague came to visit and his tyres rolled over faeces, deposited by children who were supervised by women who fried *Akara* and yam along the road. He had seen children squat several times as directed by fat women preparing *Eko* leaves to wipe the children. That was when he concluded that the kids' mothers were complicit. It was for this reason that Jide's in-laws teased him about his beloved Ibadan. He told them they would find such behaviour all around Nigeria, and that it was also because he wasn't in the urban area.

When Jide got home, Lara, his wife was bathing their baby. He got out of his damp clothes and went into the kitchen to make a cup of tea. He could have bread and tea for breakfast, lunch and dinner so long as the stuffing was different. He exclaimed when he opened the tin of milk and found it empty.

'I just got this milk. How could it be finished now-now?' Jide muttered.

Lara heard from the bathroom and answered sharply, 'How can it not have finished? Are there no people in this house?' She didn't allow him to answer; she simply went on. 'Did you buy my baby's milk?'

Jide did not like shouting in the house, so he took the empty can and went to the bathroom.

'Did you buy my baby's milk?' Lara asked again. There was something in her voice; Jide was not quite sure if it was the sharp edge of menace or the blunt edge of malice. Whatever it was, it was dripping with resentment.

'Did you ask me to buy baby milk?' Jide asked. He knew where the talk was headed and didn't like it. 'I've told you to either remind me or send me a text if there is anything to buy before I get home. It's not when I get here you start asking, "did you buy this, did you bring that?"'

'Ahan!' Lara exclaimed, 'Baba baby. Jide, how can you not know to buy baby milk before getting home, did you forget you had a baby at home? When I noticed that the baby milk had finished, I used yours.'

'For God's sake, Lara, how hard is it to send a text? How hard? Yet you keep chatting on that phone with… I don't know…but you can't send me a simple request. That's how you accused me of not buying diapers yesterday; today, it is milk.' Jide walked back to the kitchen to fix his dinner.

He slurped his tea noisily, holding the huge green mug close to his face with both hands. Lara came to meet him in the living room, holding their baby wrapped in a white towel. She thrust the baby into Jide's arms and asked him if the child didn't look like him. Jide quickly dropped his mug and held the baby at the same time; a bit of the hot liquid spilled on his trousers. He flinched; he hadn't expected his wife to drop the child on him.

'You see? You could have just burnt this girl now! You want to scald my daughter abi?'

Lara smirked and wagged her finger at Jide, telling him how every responsible man who had a family knew what to bring home.

'You didn't forget to buy your cigar abi? You come home smelling like a *mai guard* every day. Do you burn firewood at that your work? But you forget to buy things we need at home,' she nagged.

'I hope you find a job soon, Lara, so you know how it feels when you have to buy things you didn't budget.' Jide said, and immediately regretted.

'Ehen, I don't have work abi? Was I not in my father's house before you came and said you wanted to marry? Did anybody force you?'

'Lara, all I am saying is, let me know when things run out in the house on time so that I can make provision,' Jide said calmly.

The next day, Jide got off work and headed home. He stopped at the usual last shop before his turn to check if his wife had sent him an electronic list. She had: *Buy like 2k worth of tomatoes, potash, and small kerosene,* flashed on the screen. Jide ground his teeth when he saw the e-list from his wife. He had checked his phone before he left the office and didn't see it, he also checked at the traffic lights, so she must have sent it about ten minutes ago. He checked the time of message; he was right.

'I've passed the bloody tomatoes market, and who will be selling tomatoes at this time? And just what exactly is potash?' Jide said, hitting his hands on the steering. He turned the car around and drove for about ten minutes before stopping at a market where he believed he could buy the items. He felt the urge to smoke, but he didn't. He bought what he needed for the house and left. It was at the market he knew that 'potash' was used to stop tomatoes from going sour and that it also softens beans while cooking.

Jide got home to the inviting aroma of his wife's cooking. That had to be one of the best things about getting married. He had hardly cooked during his bachelor days, and when he did, he mostly swallowed the food without tasting. His routine then was bread and *akara*, bread and *moi moi,* or fish and chips for dinner. But coming home now to the smell of food made a lot of difference. It seemed like even if Lara boiled water, it tasted different. He decided not to talk about the timing of Lara's text. He didn't want to ruin a good evening.

Jide sat down in the living room catching up on the local news when Lara walked into the dining room to fill up a kettle with water from the water dispenser. She went back into the kitchen to put the kettle on a burner. Dinner was ready, and Jide grabbed a glass to fill at the dispenser. There was no water.

'Why do you boil water from the dispenser? Can't you just boil water from the tap?'

'You want my baby to drink contaminated water?' Lara replied with her hands akimbo.

'Boiling the water from the tap kills all germs you … I don't even know what to say.' Jide was frustrated. He got up; slammed the front door and went in search of 'pure water.' Jide muttered along the road, 'She could have also told me to get water on my way home. There are three dispenser kegs in the house; once two are empty, she could just simply say: please buy water. Do I have to be checking for water again? She sits at home watching Nigerian movies. She needs a job, God knows.'

Two days later, Lara called Jide to tell him that his little angel was ill and needed to go to the hospital.

'Okay,' Jide said, 'take a cab to the hospital, I'll meet you guys there.'

'Don't you think it will be hard for me to carry a baby and walk all the way to the main road to get a cab? Can't you call one of your cab guys to come and pick us from the house?'

It was times like these that Jide could swear that his wife secretly smoked something stronger than his cigarettes. He called a cab driver for her and caught up with them at the hospital. The baby was down with malaria, and the doctor prescribed some drugs, some of which were not available in the dispensary and had to be bought from a pharmacy. Lara didn't have the money to buy the drugs and told Jide to bring them home in the evening. Jide had forgot to bring his ATM card, and so could not withdraw money but he promised to buy the drugs.

There are days when forgetfulness is a plague, or Satan's tool to perform his devilry. That evening, Jide forgot to buy the medicines;

it was when he stepped out of his car and heard the wailing of his baby that he remembered. He didn't bother going into the house, he left his car and walked in search of a pharmacy. When he got in the house, he gave Lara the drugs. But she was ready for him.

'I heard you park like thirty minutes ago, but you didn't come inside because cigarette will not allow you. How can our baby be sick and all you think about is smoking like a chimney.'

Jide said nothing. She should have sent a reminder, he thought.

Jide spent his Saturday mornings washing his car. He would carefully remove parts of the car and wash them carefully. He would turn on the radio and play his R&B songs while caressing the car's interior and finally washing its body and tyres. Jide's Saturday morning was always spent that way, in that order. Once Jide finished washing the car, he checked his phone for football fixtures for the day. This Saturday, there was a midday game which looked like a big game, so he had his bath and drove to Alaba's house. From there, they would pick up Wale and go to their favourite joint, *The Monkey Guzzle* to watch the match. On getting to his friend's house, he was welcomed by Alaba who pleaded with him to wait awhile; he had to bathe two of his kids. Jide was surprised to see this. He waited for the kids to be clean, and then he asked Alaba why he was bathing the kids.

'Man, since I lost my bank job, I am more at home than my wife,' Alaba explained. 'You know she's also at a bank now. There's no point stressing that woman; she's already going through a lot. Do you know what it means for her to wake up around 4:30 am to express milk and refrigerate for the nanny to feed our baby before preparing the other child for school? Then, there is the bank wahala. Targets keep going up, and there's no promotion. Man, anyway I can help at home makes a lot of difference. Besides, we are both in this together. For now, she's the one earning a salary. Have you thought about how many sit-at-home dads there are now? Guy, it's frightening. Just among us guys, Wale, Gozie and I don't have jobs. *Things don strong for country.* It's very different from our parents' generation when men had jobs and women sat at home. *Now ehn, dem girls get beta jobs pass us o, no kidding.* They are in more professional circles than we are; they get to travel around the country and go abroad, especially those who work in HR.

'You remember Bisi, my former chic? O boy! *The babe done blow.* She is running things for one company like that. Man, I sent her my CV sharp-sharp, no dulling. If she can hook a brother up, no yawa. Because boys are roasting at home.'

Jide was silent. He stared.

'Man, the game is in like thirty minutes, when can we leave?' he asked.

Alaba explained to Jide that he had to wait a while for his wife to come back from work. 'They have Saturday banking today. She just sent me a text saying she has to stop briefly at the market, so I think I am stuck here for another hour'.

Jide did not have an hour to wait, so he called Wale. They'd both go and watch the game without the house man. For Wale, so long as there was free beer, he was ready. So, Jide left Alaba and hooked up with Wale.

The football match lived up to its rating. It was a titanic clash and bettors were sweating over their investment. Wale was frantic, checking different websites with team performances. He used current team ratings to place his bets as well as percentage odds to favour particular teams. Sometimes, he sympathised with the underdogs.

Jide did not hear his phone ring, but he felt the vibration. When he checked his phone, he saw that he had seven missed calls from

Lara. He walked some distance away from the crowd shouting instructions to players, to call her. The line wasn't clear, so Jide yelled, 'send a text, send a text.' Lara did not send a text or call back. Jide finished watching the game, dropped Wale in front of his house and went home.

'Is it that you don't want to talk to me anymore, that's why you always say I should send you a text,' Lara welcomed Jide.

'Ahan! Lara, I couldn't hear you, the line was very bad.'

'Is the line always bad when you tell me to send you a text with the list of things to buy? If you don't want to talk to me, no problem.'

'See, if you like, sulk. I did not create the telephone network. Even if I did, anything could still go wrong. I am not God.'

Jide disliked self-pity; he despised it even more when someone used it for cheap blackmail. Jide wasn't in the mood to play pacifier. He knew he should have asked about what she was saying over the phone, but he thought that if it were important, she would have sent a text or simply tell him now. Jide went into the room to change into his pyjamas; Lara went with him, talking all the time.

'Jide, sometimes I think you take too much for granted, you forget the little things that matter. If you take your time to compare yourself with your mates, you will see how privileged you are. You are the youngest among your friends, and you are almost the highest placed at work. Sometimes, I think it gets to your head and makes you arrogant. I am sure you have gone to spend good money on drinks, but if I ask you for money, you'll say you did not budget for it. All those your friends outside this house don't care about you. If anything happens to you now, who do you think will come to your aid? You better accept your world, which is this little girl and me for now, any other thing is irrelevant. Know that, before you start saying I am talking rubbish because of a simple list. Even the list sef, it's like we are in an office writing documents for a boss. Who are we documenting for? Why do you get so mad when I don't send you a message?'

Jide sat on the edge of his bed and explained; 'it's not about documentation, it's simple. If you need anything for the house, or we have run out of something, how do I know if you don't tell me? You spend more time at home and use most of these things. There are days I don't enter the store or check the fridge, so if you don't tell me, I won't know. It's just like with service standards: what gets measured gets valued. What isn't measured can't be valued'.

Lara rolled her eyes and batted her eyelids after he said this. Jide didn't like such gestures; he knew she was mocking him. But he continued. 'When you go to the market on weekends, you also carry a list of items to remind you of what you have to buy. It's the same thing I am asking for, give me a shopping list. I don't know why we get at each other because of something as simple as this, honestly. With all the work at the office, I am bound to forget what you asked for verbally.'

Lara sat. 'Remember when we went for marriage counselling before we got married? There was this resource person who took us through communication in marriage. He gave us some scenarios as role play sessions, and you laughed that that could never apply to you. I think you are behaving that way.' Jide said he didn't understand what she meant because the analogy she just played out did not register with anything concerning their marriage. She explained further.

'The resource person gave us a scenario where a woman spoke to her husband in a harsh tone because she had a better job than him. We were asked what we thought the problem was and how we would deal with it. You started talking about personality traits and the drive or lack of drive associated with such personality traits.

Most of the class did not understand you and said it was a spiritual problem the woman had; that a woman must always be submissive. I think you are forgetting my dominant personality trait and want me to conform to a strait jacket you are sewing.

Secondly, there was a couple joined by their pastor, because she believed they would suit each other. They were total strangers but both desperate to get married because of pressure. During the counselling classes, they saw that they were fooling themselves and broke up after only three weeks of dating, but they had proposed and announced they were getting married. They did not call each other during the day because they had nothing to talk about. Back then, you called me at least twice during the day and a long call at night before you went to bed. You said we could never have communication issues when we got married. Today, you tell me to send you text messages. Remember how we were also told that choosing the wrong medium for communication can also be a barrier to effective communication. Sometimes, Jide, I want to hear your voice, I don't want to text. And, seriously, don't you think this texting thing is like a dictatorship?'

Jide sat, surprised that his wife still didn't get the point he was trying to make and wondered how she had got the whole thing twisted. He was angry, but he knew anger would lead to no good. So, he tried to find a happy place in his heart and console himself by a saying. Though he couldn't remember it verbatim, he knew it went something like only boys tried to win arguments, and men knew when to concede. So, he conceded and promised to call more often during the day.

END

'SODA CANS'

Ilia's fingers fiddled idly with the third and fourth strings of the barbed wire fence; his face, pressed in the surprisingly cold wire netting, was lost in the world of the amusement park on the other side which he could only gawk at. The colours passed like a dreary blur: the carousel, bumper cars, bouncing castle, Ferris wheel; children and adults screaming their lungs out in ecstasy while having a time of their lives. His drool dribbled down a wire vine before forming a puddle in between his feet. His footwear had the soles of sneakers, but the heels and laces were strips of polythene bags he had cut up and tied.

Ilia longed for the silver trash can glistening in the sunlight like a vending machine. It spilled over with crushed soda cans, Styrofoam packs with leftover food, popcorn, straws and bottles. He could catch a whiff of the half-eaten scone and chicken wing poking out of an oily serviette. The puddle between his feet would have started to flow like a shallow stream if a park attendant hadn't come to shoo him away. The big bald pot-bellied man waved the boy off from a distance without effect; he had to rattle the fence with his baton before the boy was shocked out of his haze. It didn't make sense to Ilia that he was outside the park and he was still a nuisance. He took two steps backward to assure Pot Belly that he was leaving, then his eyes caught the crushed silver and blue can of a drink that the commercial claimed made people fly. A little bit of brown paper peeked out of the can and Ilia's heart beat in anticipation. What could it be?

Ilia was taller than his eleven years and very sinewy. His hand could easily slide through the diamond wire netting, but he knew he wouldn't reach the waste bin, so he waited for the attendant to take a turn before he dropped on his hands and knees to dig underneath the wire mesh like a dog. He was able to pull up the bottom of the wire mesh and crawl underneath before stretching out fully on the ground to retrieve the can with scratches on his head for all his troubles. The brown paper peeking from the can turned out to be a one thousand naira note. Incredible! The can slipped out of his hand and dropped to the ground. He became oblivious to the screams and music blaring behind him. He straightened out the note carefully with both hands smoothening out the creases. It was real money; his brain wasn't scrambled from being in the sun all afternoon. Ilia's mind began to race; what if someone put it there as a trap, was the owner lurking at a corner waiting to pounce on him? Where was Pot Belly? Or, could this be an enactment of some stories he had heard, of little children turned into tubers of yam after picking up money found on the ground? His legs became heavy, and he couldn't move a muscle, like a rabbit caught in the full beam of approaching headlights at night; his palms became sweaty and his fingers trembled. He cast darting glances this way and that; he became alert and threatened by the sound of birds fluttering above him, cars honking, and the sudden blast of a trumpet blown by a clown. He felt the blot of adrenaline burst, and his eyeballs widened. He bent down slowly and removed the dead hedgehogs from his feet and removed his dashiki, leaving a dirty hole-riddled singlet. He wrapped his shoes in the cloth and ran as fast as he could away from the fence, leaping over the drainage and across the road in bounds like a gazelle, car tyres screeched in his wake.

Ilia did not go straight home. He wanted to shake off whoever was tailing him, so he ran all the way to the football field in a primary school not far from his house where all the boys in the neighbourhood gathered for an evening game. There was a match against a team from another neighbourhood and the crowd standing around the field just a little away from the touchline, since there were no seats, was just what Ilia hoped. He weaved his way, slowly shuffling baby steps through the boisterous crowd from the back of one goalpost to the back of the other post, apologising to the toes he stepped on without looking up into the faces of the wincing owners. He waited for the final blast of the referee's whistle which came in two short bursts and a final long drawn blast. The field was thrown into joyous confusion as supporters of the home side ran unto the pitch to congratulate their team. The losing side left dejectedly. Ilia used the confusion as a cover and ran, full speed, all the way home.

Ilia tossed three *Akara balls* into his mouth and sipped his hot pap from a broken cup. The cup was broken by the side, reducing the quantity of liquid it could hold to about half its capacity. Ilia could swear that his mother deliberately broke the cup. He thanked his mother for dinner, as did his five siblings, and withdrew to a mat in the corner. They lived in the garage of an abandoned house; other families had carved out their spaces in the main building before his father located the property. With curtains, they divided the garage into three rooms: the children's room, the master bedroom and a living room which also served as a kitchen when it rained. This was the longest they'd stayed in a house: they had moved so often that the kids began to feel like cattle shepherded by a nomadic father. Ilia easily made friends with all the kids in every environment they stayed. He loved tyre rides, played cops and robbers with younger kids and football with older kids; his height made him fit into the older world, but most times, he liked to act like his age.

Ilia's father went out to work every morning and returned late at night, but it was the money Ilia and his five siblings brought back to their mother that she would use to prepare food for the family. All six kids scavenged refuse dumps for empty soda cans, perfume bottles and anything metallic that could be smelted or recycled. If they were lucky and gathered a fifty kg bag in a day, they could get as much as one hundred naira which they willingly handed over to their mother who stayed at home nursing the new baby.

Ilia knew no sleep that night; he kept expecting the knock on the door with the owner of the money escorted by an angry mob demanding that he be pulled out. He pictured a mob with tyre and petrol waiting to set him ablaze. He saw the mob gathering at the house whenever he closed his eyes to sleep. Whenever a rat passed, Ilia thought the mob had come, finally. Ilia sat up in bed and watched his younger ones, whisper and play under the faded Ankara wrapper that served as a blanket in the cold December harmattan. Their father occasionally barked at them to sleep before he came with his slipper. Ilia felt the urge to use the toilet, which was anywhere – behind a broken fence, under a tree or in the gutter –anyplace he could duck and ease himself away from prying eyes and passers-by. But he knew he would not go because that would mean creeping over all the sardine bodies sprawled on the mat before parting the curtain through the master bedroom.

The last time Ilia had ventured out late at night to ease himself, his father hit him so hard that he fell onto the concrete floor, crashing over the big black plastic water pitcher, which he was forced to repair.

The next day Ilia did not go searching garbage heaps or running after trucks. Instead, he walked majestically to the market area. The first shop he saw to his left had a huge glass pane displaying mannequins wearing lovely t-shirts and football jerseys. Ilia remembered once running his fingers through the polyester fabric of a red jersey worn by his coach. He loved the rubbery feel of the '8' at the back of the shirt and the name 'Gerrard' also in the same white rubbery letters. He could see himself running like the wind on the pitch, running so fast that spectators couldn't make out the name on his jersey until he had scored a brilliant goal. But for him to run that fast, he would need a pair of multi-coloured football boots like those on TV. He would also need a pair of long socks that would reach above his knees, and a pair of shin guards to go.

He looked at the price tag on the jersey and wheezed; it was six times what he had in his pocket. He dipped his hand in his pocket to make sure his cash was still there. It was. He moved to the other side of the window where he could see football boots. He said to himself, 'Since I have cash I can walk in and try them on.' He opened the door and was welcomed by sweet smelling cold air, his eyes closed for a while and a wide smile broke across his face. He got a wondering glance from the sales girl, unlike how she grovelled at another guy whose skin looked plastic. The shoes looked like something to chew on and not to be worn. The studs underneath were meant for lush grass and not the hard, undulating farm ridges they called a football field. He held the right leg and sat on a low stool gazing so hard at it until tears began to roll down both his cheeks. He would have loved to buy a pair of boots for all the boys on his team; he pictured them all running after a proper leather black and white ball and not the thing they kicked around barefoot; an orange round hard plastic float they had cut out of the toilet cistern. He also pondered about getting a team bus to ride in to their games. Ilia removed the little air freshener from the shoe box thinking it was candy that someone had dropped. It smelt sweet. He opened the pack and popped it into his mouth. A sales girl appeared suddenly and scolded him terribly, as if the stinging sensation on his tongue wasn't enough. The shoe was snatched out from his hands, and he was shoved into the scalding heat outside the shop.

Ilia felt the scalding heat anew. Being in the cool interior of the shop made him aware of the heat. He regretted popping the 'candy' into his mouth and started to spit it out vigorously when he noticed the fast food restaurant just beside him. A whole chicken was spinning gradually over a grill, dripping spicy juices with oil sizzling and sparking as drops hit the fire below. Ilia's jaw went slack. His intestines churned as he remembered the unsweetened gruel he had for dinner every day. The crispy brown sturdy chicken almost convinced him to reach deep into his pocket. There was a sharp rap on the door, and the chef came out asking how many portions he wanted. Ilia, still under the chicken spell presented his money to the chef who asked a second time how many portions he wanted.

'Meat sir, not portion.'

'My fine man, we cut up the chicken into portions. Breast into two, lower back and drumstick two, four portions in all, what would you like?'

'How much sir?'

'Six hundred per portion or do you want the entire bird?'

Ilia swallowed hard, slowly stretching out his hand to retrieve his money and returning it into his pocket.

'Can I come wash plate for you, sir?'

The chef laughed softly; he said, 'We're not hiring at the moment, but you can check back sometime.'

Ilia thanked the chef and walked away further into the market to look for fancy shirts that he and all his brothers could wear. He heard a sudden uproar of children and looked in their direction. He saw posters on the wall above the door; he dwelt on the one with a muscular soldier wearing a red headband holding a gun as big as his biceps and gritting his teeth angrily, a toothpick dangled from his lower lip. This guy must have eaten that chicken before setting out to battle, Ilia thought. The arcade with screaming children manning battle stations with control pads or joy sticks looked like heaven. He could see flawless football passes on one screen and decided that's where he was going. He noticed players with strips of paper and as soon as a game was over a young boy would punch a hole in the paper marking the number of games played and the overall cost. Ilia looked up at the posters around the arcade and could read the cost of each game. He quickly did the math of the number of holes punched for the boys practically chewing their tongues and punching away despite the blisters on their thumbs; both boys had played more than the cash Ilia had in his pocket.

'My father says gambling is not good,' Ilia muttered to himself and walked out of the arcade stealing glances at all the screens. He sat on the first step outside the arcade and held his head in his hands. He tried to think of a business to invest his money so that it could grow into something that he could use to take care of his family and friends.

Ilia hung around the market till midday when he saw his brothers at a distance fighting over who had found a pack of empty cans. Ilia felt it was funny since they never owned the returns individually.

But he understood that it was a thing of joy to be the first to find a soda can. He jumped off the staircase and ran to meet his brothers who jumped all over him in excitement. They rolled in the garbage heap trying to pin him down while one of them counted to ten like a referee in a professional wrestling match. Ilia always allowed them to win and they would run around in circles celebrating their victory. They collected scrap till late in the evening and went to trade it for cash before heading home. Because they didn't have Ilia's leadership for the better half of the day, they made only fifty naira.

Ilia washed his brothers and himself at the back of the house with water from a plastic bucket. His mother was stirring hot pap in a pot sitting on three stones with glowing coal underneath. It was a marvel to watch his mother use her bare hands to hold the sides of the pot as she stirred the gruel and adjust the coal cinders like it didn't burn her long fingers. He watched her scoop his father's food into a flask close to the man's transistor radio (the children had grown to associate the radio with their father's authority) before he approached his mother. He didn't look her in the eyes; he had never looked her in the eyes because it was rude. He towered above her now, a fact he just realised. He reached out and clasped her slim fingers. Her palm was soft and fragile. He placed the one thousand naira note in her hand and rolled her fingers into a fist; then he left to join his brothers outside. The mother, thinking it was the regular hundred bucks the boys brought back went to place the money in her safe, underneath her mattress. It was the only mattress in the house. It was used by Ilia's mother and father and a newborn until he turned two years and joined his brothers on the mat. Ilia's mother screamed, retreating from the money as if she had just seen a snake. She covered her mouth with her hands and burst into tears.

Ilia was about to exit the house when he heard his mother's

scream and rushed back to part the curtain and found her crying. She walked to him throwing her gangling arms around his neck.

'How did you get this? Return it. Please return it,' she managed in between sobs. 'Return it. We are poor, but we do not steal.'

'Somebody leave it inside soda can, Mama. I did not steal it'.

The mother paused, and then she gripped the boy by his shoulders. 'Are you sure? God bless you, my son.'

Ilia felt his mother's warm tears on his chest, and the warmth in his heart was not like the burn he got after he sipped brandy many years ago in another neighbourhood. His mother's grip tightened and he cast his mind back trying to recollect if she had ever hugged him in the past. She had not, not even after his father had flogged him with a horsewhip repeatedly for wetting the mat. He had never felt so loved. He had never seen the ocean before but heard it was blue. He noticed the colour of his mother's eyes for the first time; they were light blue like the ocean. She smelt of smoke and spice, a smell she always had. Ilia felt his mother's frail waist where his hands rested and knew why she wore so many veils. Something inside of him gave, and he began to cry. They were like that, lost in each other's embrace and didn't notice when the head of the house walked in reeking of cheap liquor.

'What? What is going on here? So, because you don't have girls, you are making girls out of my sons? You have spoilt these boys that's why they are useless,' the man barked at his wife.

Ilia watched his father take off his clothes, hang them on a nail driven in the wall then pick up his food and his radio.

END

NAVIGATION WARS

I like to think of my house as a spaceship, the kind you see in *Star Trek* with Captain James Kirk and Mr Spock and, more recently, *Miles from Tomorrow*. The ship has everything you can think of. Starting from the outer orbiter covered in a special heat shield of more than 30,000 lightweight tiles, an engine room and my special place: the control room, where we receive our routine orders and assignments from our chief galactic officer – I've never seen them in person, just on the 50-inch screen where they pop up and dish out instructions. Unfortunately, we cannot call our bosses back, like how Sports Billy calls Olympus; he can call all the time.

My five-year old son is our commander, pronounced 'kmandr', and we have to brief him first before any navigation. So, we man our different positions on the ship. The three-sitter couch is where kmandr sits with his console and the all-important steering wheel – the remote control. Fred, my husband, mans the not-too-important periscope to the left of the spaceship. While I sit monitoring the control tower, galaxy and navigation route on the virtual screen in front of me, and of course, the galley.

We've been in outer space for a couple of years now and we've almost forgotten life as it was on earth. The Milky Way is home now, and it has been fun defeating space aliens and helping others trapped in space. Until recently, our flight path was defined; we orbited soap operas. Those were times when I would sit in front of the large screen and watch my favourite soaps with a tissue box at the ready. Tear-jerkers were just so absorbing for me. I could orbit this planet for hours until Fred would come to his space station and navigate to a group of twenty-two burly men pursuing a round object. Of the twenty-men, only two could touch the round object with their hands. The others could not, except under unique circumstances. Whenever Fred orbited this world, he would concentrate and get so absorbed that he sometimes declined our galactic nourishment or delay them for later. Most times when we orbited the 22 men senselessly chasing after a small ball, I'd get busy charting our next course since his orbit lasted only 90 minutes.

Life was routine, until my stomach became a world in itself and Kmandr came to join our ship. Initially, our existence on the ship revolved around him until he came of age and in charge of the control station. After that, all we ever did was orbit a world of non-humans who sometimes sang, danced and did both sensible and not-so-sensible things. The cartoon worlds of *Blaze and the Monster Machines*, *Goldie and Bear*, and *Miles* were all we ever traversed. When we are sent into black holes by our outer galactic system and our internal light originators refuse to generate power, or when we are blown off our path by galactic winds or hit by meteorites and our transponders just won't work, Kmandr gets very bossy and I sometimes wish I could just jump ship, maybe for a while, without a tether.

Kmandr developed navigation skills at such a tender age that Fred and I could not fathom how he did it. He had learned this marvellous way of flying autopilot for periods when he would be asleep. When he finally fell asleep, and we wanted to change course, we would find that he had hidden the control console somewhere we didn't know and could not reach. We then had to walk all the way to the decoder to change course manually. Sure, we had heard of dual view and double vision, but it was not the same. I grew up with all the members of the crew manning positions in the control room with our captain dictating what course to chart without any alternate. The navigation was so much etched in our subconscious that we knew that once *Another Life* was over, it was time for bed. Back then, our journeys were time-bound, but today I sit and watch Kmandr fly the ship at any time he wants. Those of our forefather's generation would be rolling in their ancestral chairs looking down at us new age astronauts.

Our navigational challenge is not just with the path our ship flies but also within the ship. Before Kmandr came along, we could sometimes choose to walk around the ship without our space boots. Now, our feet have to be strapped on at all times. I didn't see the danger with Kmandr's playthings lying around until the day I mistakenly stepped on a miniature plastic soldier. Sarcastically, it was one of those toy soldiers with a small platform underneath their boots, so they could stand and play war. The little toy was so hard that it pierced through the skin underneath my foot and my shriek sent chills through the spaceship. I was mad that the ship scrubbing robot did not remove the toy from the control room, but I soon realised my anger was misplaced. I was the one who manned the robot all the time. Of course, robots cannot think or raise my Kmandr, and I knew I would only hurt myself if I decided to hit the robot. I don't think reprogramming would work because my operating system was way different from that of the robot. It took me a couple of frustrating trials downloading, uploading, youtubing, and trying to share software before understanding the incompatibility issues.

In our ship, I also noticed that Fred became an inventor of words, especially on the rare occasions that he and Kmandr agreed to navigate the men-chasing-ball channel. Instead of shouting 'shit!' at a missed goal opportunity, he would shout 'shiwuuut!' and 'danmdumdum' for 'damn it!' The 'F' in 'F' words was thrown away and only appeared in words like 'fire down' or 'fara bale' which is Yoruba for 'calm down.' We also started spell-talking around Kmandr, so he would not understand our conspiracies against him. It was interesting when Fred would look at me and ask, 'I feel like a C.O.K.E, what about you?' Especially at night when the little boy had to stay away from sugary foods if we wanted him to go to bed early or for our sanity at that time of the night. But we were caught off-guard pretty soon as we didn't know that Kmandr had started picking up on his spelling and found us out.

We also have to navigate through the galaxy of his wardrobe. We can't allow him wear all the bright shiny red and blue leather gear he always wants to wear. He is now aware of his shoes, which one should be for a particular activity. It's also hard to convince him to get out of his space suit in time for bed. He negotiates almost everything. I was shocked one day when I wanted to spank him for being naughty, and he looked me in the eye and coolly asked 'Mum, why do you want to spank me?' His composure shocked me more than the question. The other day, I yelled at him, and he reminded me he was just in front of me: 'Why are you shouting mum, I am right here.'

Fred and I finally realised we were the children in this ship the day I got a call from Kmandr's school teacher. I tensed up when I saw her call, because she called only when something went wrong.

She called to say that my Kmandr had insisted she call me to ask why I put *kunu*- a drink made from guinea corn - and not orange juice in his lunch box. I quickly apologised to her and pleaded with her to placate the boy. His teacher said he had refused to get back into the class after his lunch break because his classmates would laugh at him. I had to speak to him through his teacher's phone, promising to make it up to him by buying the mechanised train he longed for. The thing was too expensive for a child's play thing and I had tactfully dodged him previously on the subject. I was cornered. Trust Fred to make a joke out of everything. Till today, when I get into trouble at the office, Fred would ask if it was because of the *Kunu*.

The most complicated turn to navigate now is when I've managed to get away from Fred and Kmandr, and I'm supposed to be developing equipment with a select group of engineers, all I can think of is getting back to Kmandr and navigating through his world, or perhaps, our world – the galaxy we are building together.

END

DROLL

Crunchy potato chips crackled in Dayo's mouth; my stomach churned with violent hunger. I lay in bed facing the east with the blanket up to my neck. He sat up in bed watching *Monday Night* football on the screen to the west. I could feel his velvety skin under the sheets, and I could perceive the pleasant smell of his cologne. He had shaved before his bath.

I was upset with him when he came home later than usual. I had planned a special evening and cooked jollof rice made with gravy with loads of greens and fried chicken, and bought some ice-cream, which was still in the freezer. I yelled at his excuse and stormed off to bed without tasting a crumb. I heard him clang pots and pans and belch after filling his belly.

He still snacked on 'oniony' chips in bed to make all my senses kick, slap, pinch and bite. But I lay in bed. I should have accepted one of his three apologies earlier, but I didn't. I was being a victim of my husband's late arrival; and that, on a day when I had gone all out to impress him. I had sweet corn in a chafing dish; bacon and eggs as well; he must have wolfed them all. I licked my lips and swallowed hard. He heard it.

'Babe, are you okay?' he asked.

I ignored him.

I planned to sneak out into the kitchen after he had fallen asleep. But he must have watched the entire championship season that night. Hunger gnawed at my insides and I gripped the bed sheets tight.

He had offered a peace-offering of chocolates he bought from a hawker in traffic. It was one of those things with no word of English, which indicated cheap smuggled or dumped goods that only street boys sold. I had pretended to be vexed and stormed to the bedroom; now I could not 'unvex' just like that.

The joke was on me.

END

ACKNOWLEDGEMENTS

Many thanks to my wife, Rinret, for inspiring the collection and vigorously disagreeing with the many twists the stories initially had. Thanks to my sisters Juliette and Joy. Joy, please accept my apologies for the migraines the first draft caused you. Thanks to Ese Edah - your poem 'Insomnia' makes a difference. Obekpa Adole thanks for the many hours of discourse analysis. Thank you to Valerie Okongor, Chalya Dul, Doyin Araoye and Ema Clark. Many thanks to Ighodalo and Okhues Oziegbe and my brothers: Ayodeji, Ayodele and Ayoola.

Thank you to Professor Victor Aire, you encouraged me to get this work out with surreal mentorship sessions.

Thank you team Azafi, my publishers. Femi Ayodele 'The Editor', it was wonderful bouncing ideas off you.

www.ingramcontent.com/pod-product-compliance
Lightning Source LLC
Chambersburg PA
CBHW072028170626
46811CB00008B/2979